WARM BAGELS
& APPLE STRUDEL

WARM BAGELS & APPLE STRUDEL

OVER 150 NOSTALGIC JEWISH RECIPES

RUTH JOSEPH and SIMON ROUND

Photography by Isobel Wield

Kyle Books

First published in Great Britain in 2012 by
Kyle Books
an imprint of Kyle Cathie Ltd
23 Howland Street
London, W1T 4AY
general.enquiries@kylebooks.com
www.kylebooks.com

ISBN: 978-0-85783-054-8

Editor: Catharine Robertson
Editorial assistant: Estella Hung
Designer: Mark Latter
Photographer: Isobel Wield
Food stylist: Sonja Edridge
Props stylist: Sue Rowlands
Copy editor: Catherine Ward
Proofreader: Laura Gladwin
Index: Helen Snaith
Production: Gemma John and Nic Jones

A Cataloguing In Publication record for this title is available from the
British Library.

Colour reproduction by Alta Image
Printed and bound in China by C&C Offset Printing Company Ltd

Contents

Introduction 6

Chapter 1: Starters 12

Chapter 2: Soups 38

Chapter 3: Fish 64

Chapter 4: Meat 80

Chapter 5: Poultry 94

Chapter 6: Vegetables 108

Chapter 7: Desserts 138

Chapter 8: Cakes & Baking 154

Chapter 9: Bread 182

Chapter 10: Passover 200

Chapter 11: Pickles & Preserves 226

Jewish Dietary Laws 234

Glossary 236

Index 237

Introduction

Nostalgic memories of food are part of every Jewish existence – not simply in their minds. Remembrances of special food moments live in Jewish hearts, in their language and literature, in works of art, woven into the fabric of Jewish songs and even the lullabies Jewish mothers sing to their babies. The mere mention of a lokshen pudding can bring some Jews to the point of rapture and, certainly, nostalgia as they are suddenly transported back to their grandmother's kitchen or dining room. They have already eaten more than sufficient. And then out of the kitchen comes the stuff of dreams – a vast, baked noodle pudding, its top sugar-crusted, golden, heavy with sultanas and fragrant with lemon, loving and generous – pure theatre. She dishes an oversized portion. They protest, and then consume it with relish along with a glass of lemon tea with sugar-lumps tucked in the cheek – nostalgic perfection.

Our food memories are wrapped in a package along with framed sepia photographs, the ticking of a clock, lit candles glowing over the best china and silver and the whitest lace-edged damask cloth – other times, past lives. Our job is to preserve these important and valuable memories so they can be savoured by future generations who can go on to enjoy and recapture those wonderful moments.

Simon and I both share this passion for Jewish food and all the feelings of nostalgia that accompany each glorious mouthful. We decided to combine our mutual enthusiasm in a new book encompassing all the magical recipes of the past to preserve them for generations to come. We both write for *The Jewish Chronicle* – I am an author and now regularly contribute to the Food pages, while Simon is a Features writer. *Warm Bagels & Apple Strudel* began as a dream and evolved into a wonderful celebration of past Jewish life, both Ashkenazi and Sephardi, through a common love of food. My fascination focuses on the origins of the ingredients, plus a desire to preserve the old recipes. I have done this by recording, re-working and in some cases creating step-by-step blueprints for numerous recipes. Simon's interests evolved from interviews with his readers and their unique and individual stories of times past, resulting in their sweet remembrances of Jewish traditional foods.

We hope that *Warm Bagels & Apple Strudel* will tempt readers to remember and, in some cases, try, taste and enjoy those glorious nostalgic meals and so conserve the intangible preciousness of past Jewish life to be cherished forever.

Key to dietary symbols:

(P) *Parve* (Neutral)

(M) *Milchig* (Milky/Dairy)

(F) *Fleishig* (Meaty)

What is Nostalgia? Why Jewish Food?

The *Oxford English Dictionary* defines nostalgia as 'sentimental longing or wistful affection for the past.' And certainly food plays a major role in Jewish memory. It embraces the past like a warm coat – a source of comfort during times of sadness. Food has always played a vital role in Jewish lives. It possesses a certain magic – an intangible quality that brings different classes, different lives together to celebrate or commiserate. The best moments happen when sharing food. It may be just a good cake – perhaps a streusel kuchen, a light yeast cake flavoured with almonds and a rich buttery crumble topping, or the moistest, stickiest honey cake eaten with a strong coffee and the beginnings of conversation. It could be an invitation to enjoy a meal in a sukkah (an outside booth), created in autumn on the festival of Succoth to remember the time when the Jews wandered in the desert living only in fragile constructions that barely held off the elements. In the warmer countries of North Africa and beyond, climate is not a problem. Imagine sitting in a sukkah on a balcony or roof-top terrace, and as the decorations swing gently in the soft breezes, you listen to other celebrants singing from their roof tops. Your food may include mujadara – a delicious concoction of rice and lentils cooked together, similar to India's beloved kedgeree, decorated with a luscious layer of crispy fried onion – and a hot spiced fish redolent with spices from the Orient. Alongside them, meat- and rice-stuffed miniature courgettes. Glasses of mint tea end the meal with a slice of plum tart or a moist pastry rolled and filled with spiced dates.

Or your invitation may come from a British or North-European household. As you sit with the stars visible through interwoven branches and leaves, the thin ply walls embellished with silk hangings to give the illusion of comfort, with polished apples, pears and bunches of black and green grapes dangling from the leafy gaps, you become aware of the need for shelter and feel gratitude for the substance of your home. Wrapped in hat and gloves with heaters to warm your feet, you'll enjoy a thick soup to ward off the cold, maybe a barley soup laden with carrots and celery or white beans and mushrooms. To follow, holishkes: stuffed cabbage leaves filled with meat and rice or currants and prunes. Slices of irresistible potato kugel – a cake made by combining grated potato with onion and eggs, and then baking it until firm and golden – often accompany this meal. And everything fruity to follow: a dish of late nectarines poached in sweet wine and, centre stage, a harvest wonder of warm, spicy apple strudel, its crisp pastry topping dusted with icing sugar. Small biscuits and petit fours end the meal, along with slivers of candied orange peel dipped in chocolate. What you experience are foods devoted to sharing and still tasty the next day as a cold feast – and the understanding that every Jewish meal is tradition mixed with experiment and discovery.

Jewish food can be the glue that seals acquaintance, transforming it into companionship, often healing the breach as people sit at a table, abandoning their differences. Because of its warmth and glorious tastes it's the perfect food for welcoming strangers. There is nothing to equal the satisfying flavours of a butterbean and carrot tzimmes, which has been enriched by overnight simmering, dished generously into large bowls. Whether you make it with a piece of stewing beef and top it with a fluffy dumpling or leave it vegetarian with chickpeas and potatoes, adding extra spices, the dish will remain in your guests' recollections. Jewish food links hands across impossible barriers and draws people as one to share in a common delight. It can be the partner in the start of a relationship and, with its comforting qualities, provide support at the end. Coming together over a table to share food often eases differences far more than any heated debate.

The taste of Jewish food harks back to other times, other worlds, other countries. It holds in its heart the good, sweet essence of vanished worlds loved and lost before the diaspora. It manages to soothe the pain of past troubles by replacing them with tastes that remember all that was good and precious. That is nostalgia.

Ruth Joseph says: 'I grew up learning from my late mother, who in my eyes was the best cook in the world. She taught me how to love my ingredients, to look at a box of fresh brown eggs, one decorated with a stray feather, and marvel at their magic. Then she'd use her special alchemy and conjure those eggs with a dash of milk into chremslach, matzo-meal pancakes, or the perfect Shabbat plava, or eggy bread with a spicy sprinkling of cinnamon and sugar. I never realised that my mother was cooking on a budget – that often those eggs would form a cheap, nutritious end-of-week meal. I simply adored everything she created.

'She left me with a legacy of her passion and pleasure at making other people smile through food. That enthusiasm has never left me, and since then I have always wanted to create the foods of my childhood – to evoke that deep-rooted sweetness through my cooking and pass it on to my children and their children. I love the miraculous response of yeast to flour and water and how golden-crusted loaves of bread can emerge from a hot oven. My mother inspired me to make soup out of vegetables and pulses. I adored her perfectly crisp fried fish and moist luscious desserts, all fragments of her passionate Ashkenazi past. Her jams, pickles and chutneys, conjured out of garden windfalls, have now become part of my repertoire. Inspired by her and our Jewish heritage, I wanted to perpetuate this love of food, welcome people into my home and offer them hospitality and generosity with my own creations.

'In my case, my mother was the virtuoso of her kitchen. But in every Jewish memory there's a grandmother, aunt or mother – the balaboster – who cooked the recipes of the past. My dream is to revisit those recipes and study their origins, and then to devise a perfect step-by-step illustrated recipe so that enthusiastic cooks of the future can enjoy tastes that might otherwise disappear.'

Simon Round says: 'Had Proust been living in North London, he might well have evoked the smell of fried gefilte fish – our culinary gift to the world. The powerful scent of my mother's fried fish balls would reach my nostrils before I even crossed the road on my way home from school. And, in the kitchen, the smell would linger for days. But the taste, spiked with chraine – horseradish and beetroot sauce – made it worth the pong.

Of course, when I was a child I had no idea that 'chopped and fried' fish balls existed nowhere else in the world. In fact, it was a long time before I learned to distinguish which of my mother's recipes were Jewish and which were British or Italian. But now the smell of kosher wurst frying, the sight of chicken stock boiling for Friday night chicken soup or of fried fish with potato salad (always served cold) is the most tangible link with my past and that of my grandparents and great grandparents – this is when food nourishes not only one's body, but feeds the soul too.'

The connection with the Diaspora

Although twenty-five centuries of persecution and dispersion of the Jewish race have caused terrible pain and sadness, there have been wonderful and positive results from its scattered history. Jewish music, poetry, literature and art are all influenced by past worlds. And so is food. Jewish women took their pots and pans, and their knowledge in creating dishes, and adapted them to their new surroundings. Those Jews who fled from the Inquisition and arrived in Morocco and the Middle East discovered and learned to relish their neighbours' new herbs and spices, adding them to their repertoire. Jews who escaped the pogroms of Europe brought delicious and perfect recipes for their traditional foods as a reminder and a taste of their abandoned homeland.

It is that glorious memory – something precious tinged with an elegiac strain – that makes Jewish food so important. It carries with it a legacy of lives past, sometimes lost, but now revived and beautifully contained in this book.

Jewish Laws and Histories Shape Ashkenazi and Sephardic Cuisines

Consider the Jewish woman's situation when Sabbath restrictions forbid lighting fires and cooking by igniting a fresh flame after sunset? Some are lucky they have their own oven that will turn to a simmer so it's possible to leave food on a gentle murmur all night till lunchtime the next day. But in the past most Jews were poor and unlikely to possess their own oven. Instead the Jewish wife would give her filled Sabbath utensils and bread, specially marked with her personal identification, to the local baker who would cook them for her. Before the Sabbath or a festival she would send her children to pick up their family's food that had been simmering with the rest of the community's food. Her Sabbath bread would be cooked and a casserole dish containing her cholent, the special Sabbath stew or tagine (a type of Moroccan stew), would be brought home and kept warm,

probably swaddled in a box with blankets or hay, until the next day. Using similar ingredients to her friends and supporting market stalls that encouraged her favours, she would develop contacts and exchange confidences. Thus, through the women's breadboards and cooking pots, Jewish communities grew in knowledge and stature. Many of the recipes included in these pages originated in these very rustic utensils, baked in bakers' ovens of the past, and they evoke the scents and flavours of meals enjoyed by ancestors – still tempting, still delicious.

How easy it is for us now with our modern kitchen tools – small electric hand-whisks, mini-processors and baking parchment instead of greaseproof paper. The contrast is even more marked if we search through the Jewish heritage and look at the cooking pots and utensils

used during biblical times, when the women cooked all the food for the family, right down to grinding the flour. Only the very wealthy had a kitchen; for everyone else, cooking took place on a mud floor. The 'fireplace' was determined by a couple of stones on which a fire would be laid directly and a pot strategically placed on top. This pot would have been made out of earthenware, since metal containers and cooking utensils were reserved for the rich. Fuel was charcoal or wood cut from the surrounding land, although dried animal dung was often used as an alternative. A primitive fan was used to fuel the flames and hand-mills, fire-tongs and shovels were essential 'kitchen' utensils. Apart from these implements, no home was complete without two earthenware jugs, one for transporting water and the other for storing corn or meal. Both milk and wine were kept in goat skins, illustrating how at that time the separation of meat and milk was not yet an important factor in Jewish kashrut (dietary laws).

By the Middle Ages, famine and plague were common and it was vital to conserve every scrap of food. Preservation by pickling and salting to cure and keep, even adding honey to meats, became a valuable tool in the medieval repertoire. Surprisingly, many of these methods are still used today.

During the Diaspora at the time of the destruction of the First Temple, two main groups of Jews emerged. The Ashkenazi Jews made their way to Germany and Eastern Europe, speaking in their own dialect – Yiddish. The Sephardi Jews expanded their settlements around and beyond the Persian Empire. Some remained in Palestine and later progressed to Spain, but after persecution moved to Morocco, Italy and the Balkans. Later still these *Marranos*, as they were sometimes called, settled in Amsterdam, London and other cities.

Each time Jews moved to another part of the world, they took their pots, pans and recipes with them. Many would have been handed down from mother to daughter for her to adapt and enjoy. So we get the variations that are so fascinating and exciting within the same religion, such as pretzels and bagels. As both groups travelled, their power of storytelling, humour and song eased their anxieties

and become mingled in the mystique of the meals they cooked, which have now become narrative.

It is easy to understand how Sephardic Jewish women enjoyed their neighbours' warmth, often befriending and embracing their communities. This was partly because of climate, but also the fact that both groups cooked with vegetable oil. That meant it was possible to share some foods, even if they were basic cooked vegetables, rice, pulses and some types of bread. Consequently, Jewish families opened their doors to non-Jewish friends who were happy to return the compliment, while some Jews even began to eat food from cafés and stalls. They became more involved with the surrounding communities and found their presence tolerated to a larger extent.

In contrast, the Ashkenazi Jews lived in a cold climate, and tended to huddle together in groups and separate themselves, living totally apart. They were nervous of their neighbours, who thought them strange as they talked in a different language (Yiddish) and deliberately dressed in clothes that denoted their difference, thus enforcing their Jewishness and individuality. As a result the Ashkenazim had very little connection with the outside world and certainly never shared food, especially as the majority of their neighbours' cooking was pork-based and their cooking medium was rendered lard – certainly never the kosher Jewish chicken schmaltz. Thus the Ashkenazi Jews became isolated.

But this diversity created wonderful dishes of huge contrast – the heavier, richer cuisines of the Ashkenazim and the lighter, more highly seasoned flavours of the Sephardic kitchen. And still the Jews journeyed and explored new lands, becoming part of the communities of America and South America, China and India.

We hope to recreate for you the luscious tastes of these countries, seasoned with the essence of their surroundings, as rosewater loves cardamom, cumin and coriander. Their fragrances blend with the songs of the nightingale over a moonlit fountain, as raisins cling to cinnamon, almonds and apples hug the cosy warmth of a wood-burning stove like a shawl-wrapped Yiddish lullaby.

1: Starters

Appetisers, or *forspeisen*, are an integral part of the Jewish traditional meal. No-one would consider their Friday night menu complete without egg and onion, chopped liver or gefilte fish. And inspired by the Middle East, delicious creations from chickpeas and vegetables have now also become popular choices.

Vegetable, pulse, egg or fish starters are invaluable when devising a Jewish menu, as the rules of kashrut allow them to be served before any kind of meal, including meat or poultry (*fleishig*). Dairy starters (*milchig*) can only be served before other dairy or fish courses.

It's possible that the custom of eating something before the main course evolved from the Passover meal, where small symbolic foods are eaten with reverence. But clever mothers also created starters, usually laden with cheaper ingredients, to stifle food pangs and help to fill stomachs for less.

AUBERGINES

This extraordinary vegetable, with its tempting, polished exterior, begs to be cooked. Today aubergines are regarded as succulent vegetables, but once upon a time they were viewed with suspicion. For centuries this member of the deadly nightshade family – along with potatoes, tomatoes and peppers – was shunned by Europeans and only eaten in America, India and other distant places. Maybe the Europeans were sceptical because of the deadly nightshade connection? We know that they watched the immigrant Jews with interest, fearing if they followed their example and ate from this deadly plant they would surely go mad – hence the Italian name *melanzana*, based on the Latin meaning 'mad apple'. It wasn't until the 1500s, when the Jews were expelled from southern Italy and travelled north with their cooking pots and their knowledge of cultivation, that Europeans were finally converted. They were probably tempted by the look and fragrance of these delicious dishes, or perhaps it was the ease with which they were able to grow this prolific vegetable?

Baba Ganoush ⓟ

Traditionally the aubergines would have been roasted over a wood fire, rather like a barbecue. It is impossible to reproduce that wood-smoke taste in a kitchen, but this method still makes a gorgeous aubergine spread.

Serves 4–6

1 large aubergine or 8 baby aubergines (about 300g)
olive oil, for drizzling
coarse sea salt, for sprinkling
2 large onions, cut into quarters
2 garlic cloves, skins left on
25g fresh coriander, finely chopped
1 teaspoon ground cumin
1 tablespoon tahini paste
a pinch of paprika, to garnish
toasted pitta bread, to serve

Preheat the oven to 180°C/gas mark 4. Smear the aubergine(s) with a little olive oil and sprinkle with coarse sea salt. If you have a gas hob, place the aubergine(s) directly over the flame and chargrill the skins to blacken them. Pop the aubergines in a roasting tin, spear a few times to prevent explosion, then add the onions and garlic, and drizzle over a little olive oil. Roast in the oven for 1 hour until soft and tender. If you wish, you can peel the aubergine at this stage, although I prefer to leave the skins on to maximize the roasted flavour. Discard the stalk(s) and place the aubergine flesh in the bowl of a food-processor. Add the skinned roasted onion, squeeze in the juicy nuggets of garlic and add the fresh coriander, ground cumin and tahini paste. Blitz to a smooth (or coarse, if you prefer) paste, taste for seasoning and then spoon into a serving dish. Garnish with a little drizzle of olive oil and a sprinkling of paprika. Serve with toasted pitta bread for a light lunch or pre-dinner dip.

Aubergine with Eggs and Onions ⓟ

Like so many Jewish recipes, this recipe evolved as a cheap substitute for chopped liver and is now adored as a delicious starter in its own right.

Serves 4

1 aubergine
1 large sweet onion, peeled and sliced
3 organic free-range eggs
1 tablespoon olive oil
25g fresh flat-leaf parsley, plus more to decorate
freshly ground salt and black pepper
lettuce leaves, washed, to serve

Smear the aubergine with a little olive oil and spear a few times to prevent explosion. Grill carefully on both sides on a heated griddle pan or bake in the oven at 180°C/gas mark 4 for approximately 30–40 minutes or until the aubergine is very soft. Trim off the stalk end. Fry the onion slices in oil until soft and golden. Hard boil the eggs, then separate the yolks and whites. Process or mince two egg yolks with the onions, any remaining oil, the parsley and the soft aubergine. Grate the egg whites and add to the aubergine mixture, leaving a little for decoration. Grate the final egg yolk. Season the aubergine mix with salt and pepper. Place scoops on dishes with lettuce leaves. Add the grated yolk and white for decoration.

AVOCADOS

Although the avocado is only a recent addition to the Ashkenazi Jewish repertoire, this healthy fruit has earned its place among the treasured starters of Jewish cuisine. Adopted from its Sephardi and North American origins, it makes a welcome healthy addition to a menu that is not on the whole renowned for its vegetable content.

Avocados need to be chosen with care. They should yield slightly to the touch. If they are still firm, place in a brown paper bag with an apple or a tomato and they should ripen within about 3 days.

Avocado and Citrus Salad

Here the richness of the avocado is offset by the tartness of the citrus fruit. This is a perfect recipe to welcome the citrus season. If pomelos are not available, use pink grapefruits instead.

Serves 4

1 pomelo
2 navel oranges
1 pomegranate
1 ripe avocado
juice and grated zest of ½ lemon
25g fresh mint leaves, finely chopped
freshly ground salt

First prepare the fruit. Peel the pomelo and break into individual segments. Remove the flesh from each segment by breaking it open with your fingers. Discard the pith and place the flesh in a large bowl. Peel the oranges with a serrated knife, taking care to remove all of the bitter pith as well as the skin. Holding the fruit over your bowl, cut in between each segment to release the flesh into the bowl. Cut the pomegranate in half. To release the little jewels, hold the cut half over the bowl and bang the skin sharply with a wooden spoon. Peel the avocado, remove the stone and cut the flesh into 2cm chunks. Add to the bowl.

To serve, squeeze over the lemon juice, add the zest and scatter in the mint. Season with salt and combine well.

Avocado with Ginger and Chilli Dressing

Serves 4

juice and grated zest of 1 lime
¼ mild red chilli (pith and seeds removed), finely chopped
2 teaspoons honey
1 garlic clove, peeled and finely crushed
1cm piece of fresh root ginger, peeled and grated
15g fresh coriander, finely chopped
15g fresh mint, finely chopped
freshly ground salt and black pepper
2 avocados
4 lettuce leaves, to garnish

To make the dressing, combine the ingredients in a food-processor and season to taste. To prepare the avocados, cut them in half, remove the stones and rub the flesh with the cut lime to prevent it going brown. Arrange the lettuce leaves on four glass dishes and set half an avocado on each one. Drizzle over the dressing and serve immediately.

Variations
For a milder recipe, omit the chilli and ginger. Substitute with a teaspoon of paprika and a tiny pinch of cayenne pepper. For a summer alternative, substitute the ginger and chilli with 2 tablespoons capers, a handful of green or black olives and 1 tablespoon lemon juice instead of the lime juice.

MUSHROOMS

Eastern-European and Middle-Eastern Jews have always had an affinity with mushrooms. As hunter-gatherers they understood the value of a harvest of wild mushrooms. During medieval times, when mushrooms were regarded by the superstitious as evil (being a vegetable that seemed to suddenly emerge overnight), the Jews ignored these attitudes and used their valued knowledge and resourcefulness to provide delicious food for their families. They were grateful for the autumn mushroom harvest that came with the damp, giving a rich, substantial addition to the cooking-pot and storeroom.

Mushrooms in Soured Cream

This luxurious, rich starter would be extra delicious served with generous slices of pumpernickel bread, some sliced dill pickles or even a fresh cucumber salad. The dried porcini mushrooms enhance the woody flavour of the fresh mushrooms.

Serves 6–8

1kg wild mushrooms (or organic chestnut mushrooms)
25g dried porcini mushrooms
1 large onion, finely chopped
1 tablespoon olive oil
1 large garlic clove, peeled and crushed
1 tablespoon Kiddush wine or sherry
500ml soured cream (or Greek yogurt)
25g fresh flat-leaf parsley, finely chopped, plus a few extra leaves to garnish
freshly ground salt and black pepper
ground paprika and black olives, to garnish

Wipe the fresh mushrooms with kitchen paper to remove any dirt, but do not wash them because they will absorb the water like a sponge. Slice thickly and set aside. Cover the porcini mushrooms in boiling hot water and leave to soak for 20–30 minutes.

In a large frying pan, gently fry the onions in the oil until soft and just starting to colour. Increase the heat, add the garlic and sliced mushrooms and stir well until they start to soften.

Meanwhile, carefully strain the soaked porcini mushrooms through a piece of kitchen paper, clean muslin cloth or coffee filter paper to remove any grit, reserving the soaking liquor. Add the mushrooms to the pan, along with the soaking liquor and wine or sherry. Simmer gently for about 15 minutes until the mixture is quite firm and all the liquid has been absorbed. Set aside to cool.

Once the mushrooms are cold, stir in the soured cream (or yogurt) and parsley. Season well and spoon into a serving dish. To serve, sprinkle over a little ground paprika and garnish with olives and parsley leaves.

Mushroom Dumplings

Shavuot, with its emphasis on dairy foods, demands a celebratory recipe. Foraged mushrooms that had been pickled or dried during damp autumn days would be the ideal ingredient to add luxury to a pauper's meal. Jews from the shtetl often stuffed their mushrooms into dumplings known as *uszka*, meaning 'little ears' in Polish. My late father, who was German Polish, adored these tiny mushroom pockets served in soup or with a cream sauce. Being labour intensive, they were always a real treat on Shavuot. Even today, when mushrooms are comparatively cheap, this starter sets the tone for a special meal – adding a touch of luxury.

Makes 36

For the pastry
280g plain flour
½ teaspoon salt
a pinch of dried thyme
1 large organic free-range egg, beaten
3 tablespoons water

For the filling
100g dried porcini or shiitake mushrooms
1 onion, finely chopped
1 tablespoon olive oil
1 garlic clove, peeled and crushed (optional)
225g wild mushrooms (or organic chestnut mushrooms), finely chopped
2 tablespoons sherry, port or Kiddush wine
25g fresh flat-leaf parsley, finely chopped
2 tablespoons brown breadcrumbs or ground almonds
freshly ground salt and black pepper

Soak the porcini or shiitake mushrooms in enough boiling water to cover.

To make the pastry, place all the ingredients in a food-processor and mix to a soft dough. Wrap in clingfilm and chill in the fridge for at least 30 minutes. Wash out the processor bowl. Meanwhile, gently fry the onions in the olive oil until soft but not coloured. Add the garlic (if using) and fresh mushrooms. Cook gently over a medium heat for 15–20 minutes, or until the mushrooms are soft. Pour in the sherry, port or wine and bring to the boil to cook out the alcohol. Tip the mixture into a food-processor, add the soaked porcini or shiitake mushrooms and blitz to a coarse puree. Scoop the mixture into a bowl, stir in the parsley and breadcrumbs or almonds and mix to a firm paste, adding more breadcrumbs or almonds if necessary if the mixture is very wet. Season with salt and pepper.

To assemble the uszka, roll out the pastry as thinly as possible and cut into 7–8cm squares. Place a heaped teaspoon of the filling on each square, wet the edges with a pastry brush and fold over to form a triangle, pressing the edges to seal. (Alternatively, cut into circles and fold over to make crescents, known as pierogi.)

To cook the uszka, drop into boiling salted water or stock and simmer for 4–5 minutes. Either serve in soup broth as an alternative to knaidlach, or drain and serve as a starter with melted butter.

PULSES

Modern Jewish cooks often ignore pulses apart from their use as a soup ingredient, preferring meat, fish or eggs as an alternative. But today's thinking encourages the use of pulses, explaining that meat-based diets require seven time more land than plant-based diets. Pulses are high protein, cheap, easily stored, high fibre, low GI, and are thought to fight cancer, heart disease, diabetes and obesity. And, most of all, they taste wonderful.

During Passover, however, Ashkenazi and Sephardi Jews follow different laws regarding the consumption of *kitniot*, translated as legumes. These include rice, corn, soy beans, string beans, peas, lentils, mustard, sesame seeds and poppy seeds. The explanations are complicated, but the simplest (according to 16th-century Rabbi Joseph Caro) seems to be that planting of different crops often took place in the same piece of land. After harvesting, therefore, it was possible that the *kitniot* would be mixed with some of the grains of chametz (the five forbidden grains of Passover): wheat, spelt, barley and oats.

Falafel with Grated Cabbage Salad

Falafel is a delicious vegan recipe and it is one of the most famous street foods of the Middle East. Here the thickener is gram flour made from chickpeas, which has a more intense flavour than normal flour and makes the perfect 'glue'. Traditionally, falafel are made quite small and deep-fried, but I have made them much larger in this recipe and oven-baked them for a lower calorie, but equally tasty, alternative. The fresh parsley and coriander are not traditional but give a delicious modern twist.

Serves 2 as a light lunch or 4 as a starter with pitta and salad

For the falafel
1 x 400g tin chickpeas in salted water, drained but keeping the liquid
3 tablespoons gram flour
2 garlic cloves (or fewer according to taste – 3 is traditional and hearty), peeled and roughly chopped
1 teaspoon garam masala
1 teaspoon ground cumin
¼ teaspoon ground turmeric
pinch of cayenne pepper
1 teaspoon ground coriander
15g fresh coriander, finely chopped
15g fresh flat-leaf parsley, finely chopped
freshly ground salt and black pepper

For the grated cabbage salad
1 small firm white cabbage
2 tablespoons salt
300ml white wine vinegar
1 tablespoon sugar
1 tablespoon olive oil
15g caraway seeds
25g fresh dill, finely chopped

To make the cabbage salad, shred the cabbage finely and wash well. Place in a large bowl, sprinkle over the salt and leave to stand for 12–24 hours in the fridge.

The following day, drain thoroughly, rinse slightly and place in a serving bowl. Combine the vinegar, 300ml water, the sugar, olive oil and caraway seeds in a medium saucepan. Warm slightly to dissolve the sugar and pour over the shredded cabbage. Sprinkle with the chopped dill and set aside to cool. Chill until needed.

Preheat the oven to 180°C/gas mark 4. To make the falafel, place all the ingredients in a food-processor and blitz to a smooth paste. Set aside for a few minutes to allow the mixture to swell slightly and for the flavours to intensify. Taste and season, if necessary, with salt and pepper.

Wet your hands and roll the mixture into eight golfball-sized balls, flattened into patties. If the mixture is not stiff enough to roll into balls, add a little more gram flour and taste again to ensure the flavour is sufficiently intense. Arrange on a baking sheet and bake in the oven for about 20 minutes or until golden and crisp. Serve in pitta halves with tahini paste or harissa out of a jar, some mixed pickles and the grated cabbage salad.

Hummus

It is worth seeking out chickpeas from Asian or Middle-Eastern stores for this recipe because they are larger and more substantial. Look for ones that are tinned in salted water, as this is needed for the seasoning in this recipe.

Serves 6 as a starter or 10 as a dip

2 x 400g tins chickpeas, drained but keeping the liquid
sprig of fresh thyme (leaves only)
1 teaspoon garam masala or ground cumin
1 teaspoon paprika
2 teaspoons light tahini paste (or more for a richer flavour)
25g fresh flat-leaf parsley
juice and grated zest of ½ lemon
1 teaspoon salt
1 garlic clove, peeled (optional)

To garnish
a handful of black olives
a few sprigs of parsley

Measure out 100ml chickpea liquor from the tin and combine with the rest of the ingredients in a food-processor. Blitz to a coarse paste and spoon into an earthenware serving dish. Decorate with black olives and a few parsley leaves.

To serve, surround the bowl with washed and cut super-fresh vegetables: sticks of carrot, celery, mangetouts, baby corn and radishes.

Variations
For hummus with a kick, add a pinch of dried chilli flakes or ¼ teaspoon cayenne pepper. For pimento hummus, add 100g grilled pimentos (drained weight) and a pinch of dried chilli flakes.

EGGS

The egg is a sign of life's continuity – given to a family when a child is born and part of the mourner's meal, understanding that after death, life will return. Many Jewish communities regard the egg as an emblem of fertility – young couples are urged to eat double-yolked eggs to increase their fecundity, while some Russian Jews place a raw egg before a bride as a symbol that she may bear children as effortlessly as a hen lays eggs.

But now we know deeper reasons for the egg's symbolic importance, which extend to pre-Judaic times and were eventually absorbed into Judaism – the most interesting of those being the phoenix. For before 400BC, Herodotus, the Greek historian, talked of a mystical bird that lived for centuries, died engulfed in flames and was reborn as an egg. Jewish mystical discussions talk of a fabulous bird – the *ziz saddai*, whose wings are so large it eclipses the sun, and which will come with the Messiah and form part of the magnificent feast in the Next World. So Italian Jews place two forms of meat on the Seder table to represent the Temple sacrifices while the egg and fish show the Messianic feast of the future.

Grilled Asparagus Soufflé

I thought I'd add one modern egg recipe to the starters. Asparagus soufflés sound expensive and complicated and yet they're simplicity itself. The basic mixture can be adapted by including slivers of fresh salmon, your favourite cheese or some grilled wild mushrooms. The joy of creating a soufflé is that the sauce can be made in advance, and then when your guests arrive and are enjoying their drinks all you need to do is whisk up the egg whites, combine them with the sauce and pour the mixture into your greased moulds.

Serves 6

55g butter or margarine, plus extra for greasing
150g Parmesan, grated
225g asparagus
olive oil, for brushing
4 tablespoons plain flour
350ml milk
6 large organic free-range eggs, separated
grated zest of 1 lemon, finely grated
150g soft white cheese, such as mozzarella, finely chopped
freshly ground salt and black pepper
25g fresh flat-leaf parsley, finely chopped

Preheat the oven to 190°C/gas mark 5. Prepare six ramekins by greasing them with butter or margarine and dusting them with 50g of the Parmesan cheese. Place in a roasting tin ready for transferring them to the oven later.

Wash the asparagus and trim off the woody ends (save these for soup). Brush with oil and place on a hot griddle for 4–5 minutes until charred and just tender. Remove and leave to cool. Cut into bite-sized pieces.

To make the white sauce, melt the butter or margarine in a medium saucepan and stir in the flour. Gradually pour in the milk, whisking constantly to avoid lumps. Bring to the boil and simmer for 2 minutes to cook out the flour. Add the egg yolks, lemon zest, mozzarella, remaining Parmesan, asparagus and seasoning and stir well to combine. Remove from the heat and set aside.

Whisk the egg whites in a clean bowl until stiff. Add a spoonful of the egg white to the asparagus sauce and mix it in to loosen the mixture. Carefully fold in the rest of the egg whites, along with the parsley, and then divide the mixture between your prepared ramekins. Carefully transfer the soufflés in their roasting tin into the oven. Fill the base of the roasting tin with boiling water until it reaches about halfway up the sides of the ramekins to form a bain-marie and close the oven door. Bake for 20–25 minutes, by which time the soufflés should be risen and delicious – resist the temptation to open the oven door before they are cooked, or they will sink. Serve immediately.

Asparagus and Leek Blintzes with Y Fenni Cheese, as served to the Hairy Bikers

How many laughs can you have making pancakes? I made these for the Hairy Bikers when I appeared on their programme 'Mums Still Know Best'. We all cooked together in my home, chopping asparagus and grating cheese, and my husband and I laughed till it ached. Hopefully when you taste these Welsh/Jewish hybrids, you'll taste fun in every bite.

Serves 8–10

16–18 blintzes (see page 148)

For the filling
250g leeks, finely chopped and washed really well
1 tablespoon butter
1 tablespoon olive oil
250g asparagus, trimmed

For the cheese sauce
50g butter
50g plain flour
600ml milk
150g Y Fenni cheese (or any vegetarian Cheddar-like cheese), grated

In a large frying pan, gently fry the leeks in the butter and oil until soft but not coloured. Meanwhile, blanch the asparagus in boiling water for 3–4 minutes until just tender, or roast on a hot griddle. Roughly chop the asparagus and add to the pan with the leeks.

To make the cheese sauce, melt the butter in a small pan, stir in the flour and combine with a wooden spoon. Pour in the milk, whisking continuously for 2 minutes until the sauce thickens. Stir in the grated cheese and remove from the heat.

Preheat the oven to 180°C/gas mark 4. To assemble the blintzes, place a heaped tablespoon of the leek and asparagus mixture on each pancake and roll up. Arrange the filled blintzes in a roasting dish, pour over the cheese sauce and bake in the oven for 15 minutes until piping hot and golden. Serve with a green salad and puy lentils.

Egg and Onion ⓟ

In the past, onions were cooked with a liberal helping of schmaltz (rendered chicken fat) and a few gribenes (pieces of chicken crackling or skin) to make a dish that was super-luxurious but high in cholesterol. Present day tastes demand a lighter, healthier dish and although a good olive oil will not offer the same over-the-top richness of the past, nevertheless the combination of raw and cooked onion with good free-range eggs creates a flavourful dish that is definitely more healthy.

If you wish to follow the traditional method, substitute the olive oil for a generous tablespoon of schmaltz and a few gribenes and relish a taste of the past. Of course this will make the dish *fleishig*.

Serves 4-6

1 onion, finely sliced
1 tablespoon olive oil (or 1 tablespoon schmaltz, see page 37)
6 large organic free-range eggs
2 spring onions (pale green and white parts only – save the green ends for soup)
1 tablespoon low-fat mayonnaise
a few gribenes, see page 37 (optional – for a meaty addition)
freshly ground salt and black pepper
1 bunch fresh watercress and a few black olives, to garnish

In a small frying pan, gently fry the sliced onion in the oil (or schmaltz) until soft and just starting to turn golden. Meanwhile, hard boil the eggs for 10 minutes, drain and set aside to cool. Run ice-cold water over the eggs to prevent green edges.

Blitz the cooked onion with a hand-hand blender until smooth and scrape into a bowl. Finely chop the spring onions and mix with the puréed onion. Peel the eggs, grate them on the coarse side of a grater and combine with the onions. Stir in the mayonnaise and gribenes (if using) and season with salt and pepper. Spoon into a glass serving dish, cover with clingfilm and refrigerate until needed. This will keep well for up to 2 days in the fridge. To serve, garnish with fresh watercress and decorate with a few black olives.

Delicious Knishes ⓜ or ⓟ

Knishes are the Jewish equivalent of a pasty, wonton or tortellini – that is, a tasty filling enclosed in pastry. My mother's knishes were pillow-soft and golden with a meltingly tender filling. Like many delicacies they came about as a means of extending a precious ingredient – in this case, a sliver of meat, the last of the cheese, or some leftover spiced lentils or rice – into a delicious treat to feed an entire family. In short, this recipe conjures leftovers into the food of dreams!

There is a bit of effort involved here, but the great thing is that knishes freeze well and make wonderful party food so your efforts will be worthwhile. If you're planning ahead, make the potato filling the day before and chill it in the fridge.

Makes 24

For the dough
500g organic strong white bread flour
1 tablespoon dried yeast
1 tablespoon honey – I like the darker honey
225ml warm milk (or water)
4 tablespoons light olive oil or melted butter
2 large organic free-range eggs
1 teaspoon salt
sesame or poppy seeds, to sprinkle

For the potato filling
4 large organic potatoes, scrubbed but skins left on
225g spinach, washed really well
2 large onions, finely chopped
1 tablespoon olive oil
1 organic free-range egg
25g fresh chives or parsley, finely chopped
freshly ground salt and black pepper
½ teaspoon paprika or a grating of nutmeg

In a small bowl, combine 1 tablespoon flour with the yeast, honey and warm milk and whisk until smooth. Leave to ferment for about 15 minutes until bubbles appear on the surface. In a separate jug, combine the oil or melted butter with the eggs. Sift the remaining flour into a large bowl and add the salt. Pour in the egg mixture, add the yeast mixture and mix to a soft, pliable dough. I use my mixer with the dough hook attached. Turn the dough out onto a floured work surface and knead for 5 minutes until smooth. Place the dough in an oiled bowl, cover with a clean tea towel or clingfilm and leave to rise in a warm place for about 1 hour until doubled in size.

Meanwhile, place the potatoes in a pan of water and cook in their skins until tender. Drain, peel off the skins and mash thoroughly – or push through a potato ricer. Set aside. Place the spinach in a large pan and wilt over a medium heat. Drain thoroughly and finely chop.

Preheat the oven to 190°C/gas mark 5 and line two baking sheets with baking parchment. To make the filling, gently fry the onions in the olive oil until soft but not coloured. Add the mashed potato and spinach, along with half of the egg. Stir in the chives or parsley and season with salt, pepper and paprika or nutmeg. Tip out the dough onto a floured work surface and knead lightly. Depending on how much time you have available, there are various methods for assembling the knishes:
Method 1 (the quick method): roll out the dough to form a large rectangle, 23 x 32cm. Spread the filling over the top and roll up, Swiss-roll style. Cut into 2.5cm lengths and arrange the circles on your baking sheets with room to rise.
Method 2 (the traditional method): roll out the dough thinly and cut into 24 circles, 7.5cm in diameter – I use a large pastry cutter. Place a teaspoon of the filling on each circle, wet the edges and fold over to seal. Arrange on your baking sheets.

Transfer the baking sheets to a warm place and leave the knishes to prove for about 30 minutes until puffed up. Brush with the remaining beaten egg and sprinkle with sesame or poppy seeds. Bake in the oven for 20–30 minutes until golden. Either serve as a main course, accompanied by a watercress salad, or pass around as finger food at a party.

The Perfect Boureka

(M) or (P)

Bourekas are delicious triangular pastries similar to Indian samosas, except that the filling is not spicy. Like so many other Jewish recipes, they were born out of poverty – an expensive filling made more substantial by layers of pastry.

Bourekas make a delicious starter with a pear, watercress and walnut salad garnish. And one of the great things is you can prepare and cook them in advance, or freeze and reheat them, making them ideal for a dinner party or large buffet. Traditionally, the pastry is smeared with liberal amounts of butter, but the new way of brushing with olive oil makes a flavourful crust that is healthier and equally delicious. There are plenty of recipes for boureka pastry, many of them very complicated. However, I find bought filo pastry works just as well. I have included three traditional fillings here – potato, cheese and spinach – but feel free to experiment with your own versions.

Makes about 40 bourekas

4 x 270g packs of filo pastry
2–3 tablespoons olive oil, for brushing
1 organic free-range egg, to glaze
sesame or poppy seeds, to sprinkle

For the cheese filling (M)
120g soft white cheese, such as ricotta, mozzarella or feta
225g stronger cheese, such as Gouda or pecorino
1 large organic free-range egg
2 tablespoons natural yogurt
freshly ground salt and black pepper

For the potato filling (P)
225g mashed potato
25g fresh dill, finely chopped
25g fresh flat-leaf parsely, finely chopped
freshly ground salt and black pepper

For the spinach filling (M)
750g spinach
2 organic free-range eggs
175g Emmental, Gouda or mozzarella, grated
freshly ground salt and black pepper
finely grated nutmeg

Preheat the oven to 190°C/gas mark 5 and line two baking sheets with baking parchment. Ensure that the pastry is defrosted and ready to use.

First prepare the fillings. Grate or chop the cheeses for the cheese filling and combine with the egg, yogurt and seasoning in a bowl. Set aside. Season the mashed potato with the herbs and salt and pepper and set aside. To make the spinach filling, wash the spinach and wilt in a large pan over a medium heat. Drain in a colander and squeeze out all the moisture with the back of a spoon. Leave to cool. Roughly chop the spinach and combine with the eggs and cheese. Season with salt, pepper and a little nutmeg.

To assemble the bourekas, remove two sheets of filo pastry from the stack and cover the rest with a damp cloth to stop them drying out. Place the sheets of pastry on top of each other, cut into strips 15cm wide and brush with olive oil. Place a tablespoon of filling in one corner, fold over the corner at an angle to form a triangle and then wrap up tightly to form a neat little triangular parcel. Repeat with the rest of the pastry and fillings.

Place the filled bourekas on your prepared baking sheets, glaze on both sides with beaten egg and sprinkle generously all over with sesame or poppy seeds. Bake in the oven for 15–20 minutes until golden brown.

Variations
Include slivers of brie instead of soft white cheese, or some chopped nuts or pimentos for extra flavour. To liven up the potato filling, add a handful of chopped olives, a tablespoon of pesto sauce or some sliced and fried mushrooms or onions.

ARTICHOKES

Artichokes with Lemon Mayonnaise ⓟ

This fascinating member of the thistle family was known by the ancient Greeks and is said to have originated in Sicily. As a vegetable it has always been venerated as something special. Charlemagne insisted it was grown in his gardens, though his citizens never shared his passion for the thorny vegetable. When Catherine de Medici brought the plants to Europe, she was considered a woman of easy virtue, since artichokes were known to have aphrodisiac properties. Marilyn Monroe won the title of California's Miss Artichoke!

When Jews were incarcerated in the Italian ghettos, artichokes came to be known as the Jewish vegetable, because Jews would consume them in large quantities, being one of the few cheap vegetables available.

They are very healthy, providing generous amounts of vitamin C, magnesium, folic acid and dietary fibre.

Serves 6 as a starter

6 globe artichokes
juice of ½ lemon
1 onion, roughly chopped
2 garlic cloves, peeled and left whole (optional)

For the lemon mayonnaise
1 organic free-range egg yolk
225ml olive oil
freshly ground salt and black pepper
1¼ tablespoons lemon juice

Clean the artichokes carefully by washing behind the open leaves. Trim off and discard the first set of outer leaves and the stalk. Place in a pan of boiling water (just enough to cover), add the lemon juice, onion and garlic (if using) and simmer for 30 minutes, or until the leaves easily come away from the stem.

Meanwhile, make the lemon mayonnaise. The easiest way to do this is in a food-processor. Place the egg yolk in the bowl of the processor, switch on the blade and carefully dribble in the olive oil a few drops at a time through the feeder tube. As the mayonnaise starts to thicken, you can add the oil more quickly until it has all been amalgamated. If you don't have a processor, simply whisk the egg yolk in a bowl and add the oil very slowly – one drop at a time to begin with – whisking all the time. As before, once the mayonnaise thickens you can trickle in the oil more quickly. Season with salt, pepper and a generous squeeze of lemon juice. The perfect seasoning is actually the juice left over from a jar of sweet and sour pickled cucumbers. Add until you have the right texture and you will find that this gives exactly the right level of acidity to your mayonnaise.

Drain the artichokes and place one on each plate. If you wish, you can cut them in quarters and remove the fine choke needles. This will make eating easier as guests can then pull away at the fleshy ends of the leaf and finish with the delicious nutty hearts. Serve with the lemon mayonnaise on the side.

Roman Fried Artichokes ⓟ

Artichokes have long been part of the Italian repertoire. One classic recipe, Jewish Artichokes or *Carciofi alla Guidia*, is so ancient that it is said to have originated during Roman times. As usual the Jewish woman used her ingenuity to convert a relatively cheap product into a fabulous delicacy.

This recipe breaks with tradition as the artichokes are poached first, then fried. This way they are always tender, and the chokes can be removed more easily for a better and more successful result. Also, less oil is absorbed when the artichokes are fried.

Select young artichokes with closed petals for this as the younger buds are tender and have more flavour. Don't overcook them – they are done when the tip of a knife or fork slides in easily. Use a stainless steel pan to boil the artichokes in, as iron or aluminium pots will blacken them.

Serves 6 as a starter

6 baby artichokes
juice of ½ lemon
freshly ground salt and black pepper
vegetable oil, for deep-frying

Prepare the artichokes by removing any tough outside leaves and trimming the tips. Place the artichokes in a large saucepan and cover with boiling water. Add the lemon juice and simmer for 15 minutes, until tender but not soft. Drain thoroughly.

Leave to cool slightly, approximately 10 minutes. With a small sharp knife, make two vertical diagonal cuts into the centre of each artichoke, removing the fine needles within the choke with a spoon, leaving a hollowed-out centre and retaining all the delicious base. Rinse well and pat dry using kitchen paper or a clean tea towel.

Preheat the oil to 170°C in a deep-fat fryer (or half fill a large saucepan with oil, and heat until hot but not smoking.

Lay a clean tea towel on your work surface and arrange the drained artichokes, face down, on top. Press down firmly on the base of each artichoke so that the petals fan out into a flower shape. Season well with salt and pepper.

To fry the artichokes, carefully ease them into the hot oil and fry for 10–12 minutes, until golden. You might need to do this in batches. When cooking for a dinner party use two pans. Drain on kitchen paper. Keeping the artichokes well away from the hot oil, immediately sprinkle each one with a little cold water – this will make them crisp up – and serve straight away. Serve with a Caper and Garlic Vinaigrette.

Caper and Garlic Vinaigrette

Combine 1 clove crushed garlic, 75ml red or white wine vinegar (whichever you prefer), 2 tablespoons chopped capers in brine, 225ml olive oil, 2½ tablespoons runny honey and freshly ground black pepper.

HERRINGS

The beginning of the 19th century saw advances in sea and land transport and the development of a new society of Jewish merchants who exported their wares to the people of Eastern Europe, from Holland, Scotland, Norway and England. One of their main exports was the herring – a cheap, nutritious, plentiful form of food, easily preserved by smoking, salting and pickling. Consequently the herring became the focus for many Jewish Ashkenazi diets. Along with a plain boiled potato, cabbage, bread and pickles, it became standard fare. Now its traditional flavour, adored by many, is redolent of sweet times past.

Chopped herring

Serves 4–6

4 salt herrings (or 4–5 pickled herrings from a jar)
3 organic free-range eggs
2 thick slices of stale challah or white bread
1 medium sweet onion, roughly chopped
1 small Bramley cooking apple, peeled and cored
1 small eating apple, peeled and cored
1 tablespoon white wine vinegar
1 tablespoon olive oil
½ teaspoon sugar, to taste
2 tablespoons ground almonds (optional)
1 pickled cucumber, grated (optional), plus extra to garnish

If using salt herrings out of a barrel (rare these days), soak them in cold water overnight. Skin and bone them, taking care to remove all of the bones. If using herrings out a jar, simply remove the tails and any fins. Don't worry about washing them.

Hard boil the eggs for 10 minutes, then drain and run ice-cold water over the eggs to prevent green edges. Set aside. Place the bread in a food-processor, process into fine crumbs and tip into a bowl. Add the herrings and onion to the food-processor and blitz to a smooth paste. Scoop into the bowl with the breadcrumbs. Grate the hard-boiled eggs on the coarse side of a grater and then grate the apples. Fold the grated egg and apple into the herring mixture, along with the rest of the ingredients. The grated pickled cucumber (if using) will give the dish a sharper taste. Serve on small squares of pumpernickel bread with a sliver of dill pickle to garnish.

Chopped Liver

Our Friday night chopped liver was not just the start of another memorable meal but was also part of the Sabbath celebration. My late mother gave the preparation as much covet – importance or respect – as the main course. She used a few saved and koshered chicken livers, carefully extended with a mound of sweet fried onions, simmered gently with a little schmaltz and a handful of homemade gribenes and hard-boiled eggs. She'd mince it all together in an old-fashioned Spong mincer, clamped to the Formica tabletop, apart from one egg which was left to be grated carefully over the served mounds of liver – yolk and white separate. Finally the mixture was combined and, on extra-special occasions, moistened with a little Kiddush wine already sitting next to the polished candles. The chopped liver was then served in generous mounds on small glass plates from Woolworths and decorated with the egg and circles of pickled cucumber.

Serves 6–8

450g chicken livers, trimmed
  (remove any green spots carefully)
5 organic free-range eggs
2 large onions, sliced
1 tablespoon olive oil
  (or 1 tablespoon schmaltz, see below)
a few gribenes (optional), see below
25g fresh flat-leaf parsley, finely chopped
2 tablespoons Kiddush wine, brandy
  or chicken stock
freshly ground salt and black pepper
a little paprika, to garnish

If you are using raw chicken livers, you will need to kosher them according to the Jewish law so that every scrap of blood is removed. In order to do this, it is necessary to salt the livers first to prepare them for grilling. Carefully line the bottom of the grill with kitchen foil to catch any drips of blood. Then, using tongs, hold the slices directly over a gas flame until they are virtually cooked. Some of the outside edges will be almost burnt but this charring seems to enhance the flavour of the dish.

Hard boil the eggs for 10 minutes, drain and set aside to cool. In a large frying pan, gently fry the onions in the oil (or schmaltz) until soft and golden. Increase the heat, add the koshered livers and stir for a few seconds so that they absorb the flavour of the onion. Either tip the mixture into a food-processor and blitz to a coarse or smooth paste with the gribenes (if using), or pass the mixture through an old-fashioned mincer. Scoop into a bowl. Grate the eggs on the coarse side of a grater and add to the bowl, reserving a little of the grated egg for the garnish. Stir in the parsley and fold in gently. Moisten the mixture with some wine, brandy or chicken stock and season to taste with salt and pepper. Cover with clingfilm and chill until needed. Serve in scoops on individual plates topped with a little grated egg and paprika for colour, and generous pieces of fresh Friday-night challah.

To make gribenes and schmaltz

Remove the spare fat from a raw chicken and place in a pan. (There is usually a lump of fat around the neck, in an older bird at least.) Add 250g dairy-free margarine, 1 teaspoon salt and 1 large onion (with the skin left on to enhance the golden colour). Remove the skin from the chicken, cut into smallish pieces and add to the pan. Set over a very low heat and cook for 1½–2 hours until all of the fat has been rendered gently out of the chicken skin. Remove the skin from the pan and drain on kitchen paper to form gribenes or crackling. Pour the fat (schmaltz) into an earthenware or heavy-duty glass dish and store in the fridge until needed*. As the fat cools, a rich jelly will collect at the bottom of the dish. This forms a delicious base for soup or sauces.

* The fat (schmaltz) will keep for up to 6 weeks in the fridge. Store the gribenes in the fridge.

2: Soups

Winter or summer, soup plays a vital part in a Jewish meal. Traditions began with the biblical 'mess of potage' mentioned in Genesis and sold by Jacob to Esau. At that time, cooking methods were primitive and involved simmering pieces of meat, chicken, fish, lentils and grains in a clay pot with water and vegetables over an open fire.

Chickens had been kept by man since prehistoric times and communities cooked the capons and older birds by simmering them in water – tenderising parts that would otherwise be discarded. Throwing away the liquid was wasteful and gradually the liquid became as important as the contents. It was Maimonides (1135–1204), rabbi, philosopher and physician, who recommended chicken soup as nourishing for invalids – and so the belief that chicken soup has magical powers was born. Today, it is still described as 'Jewish penicillin'. Gradually the curative chicken soup idea merged with the importance of the Sabbath, and Jewish communities adopted chicken as the focus of their Shabbat meal – especially as it tolerated an overnight simmer. A custom also evolved in many communities to serve chicken soup at weddings, since the yellow fat 'eyes' were said to be symbols of money and future prosperity.

While chicken soup plays a vital role in Jewish culture, not all traditional soups include chicken. The poor Jews of Eastern Europe created 'Soup mit Nisht' (soup with nothing), containing neither fat nor meat, but with cabbage, potatoes or beetroot for the base. And so, paying homage to our Jewish soup past, we offer you traditional soups and a few new, easy-to-make soups for the best comfort food. Unless specified, most of these soups have a vegetarian base which keeps them parve. However, you can easily modify them by adding a beef bone, some chicken meat or chicken stock.

Jewish Penicillin Vietnamese style ⓕ

We love chicken soup – that warming and reviving broth that is reputed to have medicinal properties. But other cultures do chicken soup too (some of them surprisingly similar to our own), so when you become tired of Jewish penicillin, try this adaptation of Vietnamese pho ga. It will seem oddly familiar – but in a zingy kind of a way.

Serves 4

6 chicken thighs (with skin and bone left on)
2.5cm piece of fresh root ginger, peeled
3 garlic cloves, peeled
1 piece of lemongrass
1 cinnamon stick
1 star anise
1 chicken stock cube
2 tablespoons soy sauce
300g vermicelli or lokshen noodles

To serve
a handful of mixed fresh herbs (ideally mint, coriander and Thai basil), finely chopped
2 spring onions, finely chopped
a handful of beansprouts, to garnish
juice of 1 lime
1 green chilli (seeds removed), finely chopped (optional)

Place the chicken pieces, ginger, garlic and lemongrass in a large saucepan and fill three-quarters full with cold water. Bring to the boil, and then reduce to a simmer and skim off any scum from the surface with a spoon. Add the cinnamon, star anise, chicken stock cube and soy sauce and simmer for 45 minutes to an hour. Remove from the heat.

Take out the chicken pieces and set aside on a plate. Discard the ginger, garlic, lemongrass and whole spices. When the chicken is cool enough to handle, remove the skin, cut the flesh from the bone and divide it between four bowls. Bring the broth back to the boil, add the vermicelli or lokshen noodles and cook according to the packet instructions. Ladle the soup and noodles into the bowls and garnish with the herbs. Serve with spring onions and beansprouts, plus lime juice and chilli to taste.

Watercress and Baby Leek Soup

(P) **(with optional milky garnish)**

This extra-light, easy-to-prepare soup tastes wonderful and is choc-full of glorious nutrients.

Serves 6

400g baby leeks, trimmed,
    washed and roughly chopped
2 small onions, finely sliced
1 tablespoon olive oil
2 large potatoes, scrubbed and
    cut into rough chunks (skins left on)
850ml vegetable stock
200g fresh watercress
freshly ground salt and black pepper
fromage frais (optional), to serve

In a large pan, gently fry the onions and leeks in the olive oil until soft. Add the potatoes and stock, along with the watercress stems, and simmer for 15–20 minutes until the potatoes are tender. Tip into a food-processor, add the watercress leaves (reserving a few for decoration) and blitz until smooth. Season to taste with salt and pepper. Ladle into soup bowls and add a swirl of fromage frais (if using). Garnish with the reserved watercress leaves and enjoy in good health.

Cauliflower and Onion Soup Ⓟ

The creamiest, quickest, cheapest slimming soup in the world! This is the modern-day equivalent of 'Soup mit Nisht', a low-calorie soup that will fill you up on the cheap. This delicious soup can be made in minutes if you have a pressure-cooker and a food-processor.

Serves 4

2 large onions, peeled and finely sliced
1 tablespoon olive oil
900g cauliflower florets (frozen is fine)
900ml vegetable stock
25g fresh flat-leaf parsley
freshly ground salt and black pepper

In a pressure cooker or large pan, gently fry the onions in the oil until soft. Add the cauliflower, pour in the stock to cover and bring to the boil. Simmer gently for 5–10 minutes, or until the cauliflower is very soft. Pour into a food-processor, add the parsley and blitz until smooth. Season with salt and pepper. Serve as a light lunch or delicate starter.

Variation
For a soup rich in folic acid and iron, remove the stalks from one bunch of watercress and add to the pan with the cauliflower, onions and stock. Place the leaves in a food-processor with the parsley and blitz until finely chopped. Pour in the cooked cauliflower soup and blitz again until smooth. Season well.

Mushroom and Barley Soup Ⓟ

Also known as *krupnik*, this traditional Polish/Russian/Lithuanian soup is rich in comforting flavours. If possible, use the traditional dried porcini mushrooms for a darker flavour and colour.

Serves 6 hungry people

25g dried porcini mushrooms
125g pot barley (barley with the husks left on and higher in fibre; if unavailable, use 125g pearl barley)
1.2 litres vegetable stock
1 large onion, finely chopped
1 tablespoon olive oil
2 carrots, peeled and finely chopped
2 celery sticks, trimmed and finely chopped
1 medium potato, scrubbed and finely diced (skin left on)
freshly ground salt and black pepper
25g fresh flat-leaf parsley, finely chopped

Soak the dried mushrooms in 750ml hot water. Meanwhile, cook the barley in the stock according to the directions on the packet. (The easiest way is to place the barley and stock in a glass dish with a lid and microwave it on high for 50 minutes.)

Drain the mushrooms, keeping the soaking liquid, and finely chop them. In a large pan, gently fry the onion in the olive oil until soft. Pour in the cooked barley along with the stock. Add the mushrooms with their soaking liquid, throw in the carrots, celery and potato and bring to the boil. Turn down the heat and simmer gently for 15–20 minutes until the vegetables are really tender and the barley has released its creamy texture. Add more stock, if necessary. Season with salt and pepper, stir in the parsley and ladle into soup bowls. Serve with chunks of rye bread and pickled dill cucumbers.

Variations
For a milky meal, replace 750ml of the vegetable stock with 750ml skimmed milk. For a meaty meal, replace the vegetable stock with chicken stock and include some cooked chicken at the end, if you prefer. For a more substantial meat soup, simmer the vegetables with a beef bone for 30 minutes and stir in some tinned butter beans at the end.

Butter Bean and Barley Soup ⓟ

This hearty soup is a nutritionists' dream – those Bubbas certainly knew how to feed their families! By combining a pulse with a grain and adding vegetables they were providing their families with a perfectly balanced, meatless meal – although often a piece of stewing meat or bone would have been added for extra flavour.

Serves 8–10

100g pearl barley
2 medium onions (about 400g), finely sliced
1 tablespoon olive oil
500g potatoes, scrubbed and cut into chunks (skins left on)
200g carrots, peeled and roughly chopped
200g leeks, roughly chopped and washed really well
200g celery, roughly chopped
2 vegetable stock cubes
1 x 410g tin butter beans in water, drained
1 x 410g tin borlotti beans in water, drained
25g fresh flat-leaf parsley or coriander, finely chopped
freshly ground salt and black pepper

Place the pearl barley in a saucepan, cover with twice the volume of water and simmer for 60 minutes until very soft and creamy. Top up the water if necessary if it starts to dry out. (Alternatively, cook in the microwave for 50 minutes.)

In a large pan, gently fry the onions in the olive oil until soft. Add the vegetables and cover with boiling water. Crumble in the stock cubes and stir to dissolve. Tip the cooked pearl barley, along with the cooking liquid, into the pan and simmer for about 20 minutes, or until the potatoes are cooked and the vegetables are tender. Add the tinned beans and the chopped herbs, season with salt and pepper and ladle into soup bowls.

Variations
For a hearty, meaty meal, sweat the onions and remove them from the pan. Increase the heat and fry 1kg stewing meat (shin or brisket) until brown all over. Return the onions to the pan with the (uncooked) pearl barley. Cover with water, add the stock cubes and simmer for 45 minutes, stirring occasionally. Add the vegetables, along with the tinned beans, and simmer until all the vegetables are tender. Stir in the chopped herbs and season to taste. Just before you are about to serve, remove the meat from the pan and cut into bite-sized pieces. Place the meat in your soup bowls and ladle over the soup.

For a warming, spicy soup, add 1 teaspoon mustard or caraway seeds and 2 chopped garlic cloves with the onions. Stir in 2 tablespoons raisins and the grated zest of 1 lemon with the stock.

Tomato Rice Soup

Traditional Tomato Rice Soup – made by simmering fresh or tinned tomatoes with stock, processing with herbs and adding leftover cooked rice – has always been a Jewish favourite.

Mervyn's Roast Tomato Soup

I arrived at this fabulous easy-cook soup after experimenting with a glut of glorious vegetables from my husband Mervyn's greenhouse. If you haven't got a green-fingered husband, these vegetables are all in their prime in early autumn, making this a perfect starter for a Rosh Hashanah milky meal. This soup is super healthy, with its cooked tomato lycopene content; the onion and garlic work wonders for the immune system.

Serves 4–6

1.5kg fresh tomatoes, cut in half
2 large onions, cut into rough chunks
   (skins left on)
1 large red pepper, cut into rough chunks
   (seeds and white pith removed)
1 garlic clove, crushed but left whole (optional)
1 chilli, split in half and seeds removed (optional)
1–2 tablespoons olive oil
freshly ground salt and black pepper
100g organic short-grain brown rice
25g fresh basil
900ml vegetable stock
1 teaspoon brown sugar
1 tablespoon ground paprika

Preheat the oven to 190°C/gas mark 5. Place the tomatoes, onions, red pepper, garlic and chilli in a large roasting tray. Drizzle over the oil, season with salt and pepper and roast in the oven for 40 minutes. Remove from the oven and set aside until cool enough to handle.

Meanwhile, cook the rice according to the instructions on the packet and drain well. (I cook it in the microwave.)

Once the vegetables are cool enough to handle, carefully remove the skin from the onion and squeeze out the roasted flesh from the garlic. Place the onion and garlic flesh in a food-processor, along with the roasted vegetables and basil, and blitz to a coarse paste. Alternatively, chop everything finely by hand. (If you wish you can remove the skins from the tomatoes, but we leave them on for added fibre.) Scoop the vegetable purée into a pan and pour in enough stock to make a soupy consistency. Add the cooked rice and stir over a low heat for 2–3 minutes until combined. Season to taste with salt, pepper, a teaspoon of sugar and paprika. Serve with thick sourdough toast and fresh hummus on the side.

Variation
For a less spicy soup, omit the chilli and substitute some of the stock for milk or soya milk to give a creamy texture.

Haimishe Potato Soup

(P) **(with optional milky garnish)**

Eastern-European Jews probably owe their existence to the humble potato. Previously they depended on unreliable crops of rice, buckwheat, millet and pulses, made into a type of runny porridge, to carry them through their frozen winters – and numerous generations perished with poor harvests. However, under Catherine the Great, the peasant population were encouraged to settle in the fertile lands of the Ukraine and Middle Volga and ordered to plant potatoes. In 1850, Tsar Nicholas I, Catherine's son, enforced this edict and potato production doubled – while the Jewish population quadrupled in numbers! At last their diet included a nutritious carbohydrate alongside a little rough bread and other vegetables such as cabbage and carrots, pickles, an occasional herring or very rarely a chicken.

Potatoes contain fibre, ascorbic acid (vitamin C) and minerals – in fact, every necessary nutrient except vitamin A, vitamin D and calcium. This soup is a typical offering and its milky garnish provides a modern colourful twist.

Serves 4–6

1 large onion, finely chopped
1 tablespoon olive oil
3 garlic cloves, peeled and finely chopped or crushed
500g potatoes, scrubbed and cut into chunks (skins left on)
3 large carrots, peeled and roughly chopped
2 celery sticks, finely chopped
1.2 litres vegetable stock
1.1 litres soya milk (or more stock for a lighter flavour)
freshly ground salt and black pepper
25g fresh flat-leaf parsley, finely chopped
10g fresh dill, finely chopped

To garnish (optional)
150ml soured cream or low-fat Greek yogurt
25g fresh dill, finely chopped
1 teaspoon caraway seeds

In a large pan, gently fry the onions in the olive oil until soft. Add the crushed garlic and stir to release the flavour. Add the potatoes, carrots and celery and pour in the stock to cover. Bring to the boil, and then simmer gently for about 25 minutes until the vegetables are tender. Allow to cool slightly. Meanwhile, toast the caraway seeds in a dry pan over a low heat until they release their aroma.

Pour the soup into a food-processor, add the milk and blitz until smooth. Season with salt and pepper and stir in the chopped parsley and dill. Ladle the soup into bowls and add a swirl of soured cream on top. Sprinkle with dill and toasted caraway seeds and serve with pumpernickel sticks. Accompany with a radish, apple and watercress salad and either a sharp cheese for vegetarians or some pickled herring.

Variation

For potato and mushroom soup, soak 40g dried porcini mushrooms in 2 tablespoons water (or sherry) for 20 minutes. Process the soup and return it to the pan. Add the strained mushroom liquid, along with the chopped mushrooms and simmer gently for a further 15 minutes. Omit the dill and soured cream topping.

Easy Red Lentil Soup

Historically, lentils have always been part of the Jewish diet. Archaeological evidence in Ein Gedi shows that lentils were growing during Chalcolithic times. And in the Mishnah – the first written laws – it says that if a man separates from his wife, then a portion of her separation allowance is paid in lentils! We also know that a type of lentil flour was incorporated into the first biblical bread.

Serves 4–5

250g red lentils
1 litre vegetable stock
1 large red onion, peeled and finely chopped
4 large carrots, peeled and finely chopped
3 celery stalks with leaves, finely chopped
1 tablespoon olive oil
freshly ground salt and black pepper

Place the red lentils in a large glass casserole dish, cover with half of the stock and cook in the microwave for 30 minutes on high until really tender. (Alternatively, simmer gently in a pan on the hob until tender, topping up with water as necessary to stop them drying out.)

In a separate, large pan, gently fry the onions, carrots and celery in the oil until just starting to soften. Add the remaining stock and simmer for about 15–20 minutes until the vegetables are completely tender. Add the cooked lentils, along with their cooking liquid, season with salt and pepper and stir over a low heat for a few minutes until everything has amalgamated.

Variations

For tomato and lentil soup, add 1 x 400g tin chopped tomatoes, 1 teaspoon tomato purée and 1 heaped teaspoon paprika with the remaining stock. Simmer for 20 minutes before adding the lentils.

For a hearty, aromatic soup, use green or brown lentils instead of red lentils and include 2 large parsnips, peeled and chopped with the vegetables and 2 generous teaspoons garam masala. Stir in 25g finely chopped fresh coriander at the end.

Sephardi-style Harira Soup (P)

Moroccan Jews have adopted their neighbour's national soup. As this soup takes time to make it's worthwhile making double, especially as it freezes well and tastes even more luscious on reheating. Normally it contains a little whisked-in flour and some noodles, but I have replaced these here with brown rice and extra vegetables for a super-healthy version.

Serves 4–5

120g red lentils
100g organic short-grain brown rice
1 large onion, finely chopped
1 tablespoon olive oil
2 celery sticks, finely chopped
1 large leek, trimmed and finely chopped
2 large carrots, peeled and finely chopped
1 tablespoon tomato purée
a pinch of ground saffron (or saffron strands)
¼ teaspoon ground ginger
1 teaspoon paprika
¼ teaspoon ground black pepper
a pinch of cayenne pepper
1 teaspoon sugar
1 x 400g tin chickpeas, drained and rinsed
1 x 400g tin chopped tomatoes
25g fresh flat-leaf parsley, finely chopped
25g fresh coriander, finely chopped
freshly ground salt, to taste

Place the lentils and rice in a glass bowl, cover with 900ml water and cook in the microwave on high for about 30 minutes until tender. (You can do this on the stove, but you will need to top up the water level from time to time to stop the lentils from drying out.)

In a pressure cooker (if possible) or large pan, soften the onions in the oil. Add the celery, leeks, carrots, tomato purée, saffron, ginger, paprika, black pepper, cayenne pepper and sugar and give everything a good stir to coat the vegetables in the oil and spices. Pour in 2 litres water, bring to the boil and simmer for about 15 minutes or until the vegetables are tender. Add the cooked lentils and rice, along with the drained chickpeas and tinned tomatoes and simmer for 5–10 minutes to heat through. Sprinkle in the herbs, stir to combine and season with salt to taste.

Variations
For a meaty version, stir in some diced stewing steak or lamb neck bones with the vegetables and simmer for 45 minutes–1 hour, or until the meat is tender and falls off the bone.

Onion Soup

This delectably satisfying soup imitates a rich French onion soup. Use large sweet Spanish onions in their prime and cook them slowly until meltingly soft for a deeper flavoured soup.

Serves 4–6

6 large Spanish onions, finely sliced
3 tablespoons olive oil
2 garlic cloves, peeled, green part removed and crushed with 1 teaspoon salt (add more if necessary as sometimes the onions are very sweet)
900ml strong vegetable stock
50ml good red wine
a dash of brandy or Kiddush wine (optional)
25g fresh flat-leaf parsley, finely chopped
freshly ground salt and black pepper

For the croûtons
3 thick slices of sourdough bread, cut into 3cm squares
2 tablespoons olive oil
1 tablespoon ground paprika, to sprinkle

Place the onions in a large pan with the olive oil and set over a very low heat. Cover the pan with a lid and sweat gently for about 20 minutes until the onions are almost tender, stirring occasionally. Add the crushed garlic and salt and continue cooking until the onions are golden brown and meltingly soft. Pour in the vegetable stock, red wine and brandy or Kiddush wine and bring to the boil. Turn down the heat and simmer with the lid off for about 10 minutes.

Preheat the oven to 170°C/gas mark 3 and line a baking sheet with baking parchment. Brush the bread squares with olive oil and sprinkle with paprika. Bake for about 30 minutes, turning once, until the croûtons are crispy and golden.

Once the soup is cooked, stir in the parsley, season with salt and pepper and ladle into soup bowls. Serve with the croûtons floating on top.

Variations
For a thicker, creamier soup without the alcohol, substitute the wine with an extra 50ml vegetable stock and add 1 large potato, cut into chunks. Simmer the soup very gently for 5 minutes, taking care it doesn't boil over. Then blitz in a food-processor with the parsley and seasoning.

For cheesy croutons
Cook the bread squares in the oven for 25 minutes, and then sprinkle them with 70g grated cheese of your choice – Gruyère or pecorino are delicious. Put them back in the oven for the remaining 5 minutes. Then serve in the hot soup – remember this makes it *milchig*.

For a meaty soup, omit the cheesy croûtons and substitute the vegetable stock with meat stock.

BORSCHT

Borscht or beetroot soup was the backbone of many Ashkenazi cooks' repertoires and served as a valuable filler in leaner times. The meaty version usually contained a bone or a piece of stewing beef, according to the family's finances, to be boiled with the beets.

Vegetarian Borscht (P) (with optional milky garnish)

This substantial summer soup is a meal in itself.
Serves 4–6

10 small beetroot, peeled and finely chopped
1 large onion, finely chopped
1.2 litres vegetable stock (or water)
3 medium potatoes
4 organic free-range eggs
1 lemon
1½ tablespoons sugar
1½ teaspoons salt
25g fresh flat-leaf parsley, finely chopped
25g fresh dill, finely chopped – save a few fronds for decoration
1 teaspoon caraway seeds
soured cream, to serve

Place the beetroot and onions in a large pan, cover with the stock or water and simmer for 15 minutes. Meanwhile, in a separate pan, boil the potatoes in their skins until soft, and in another pan, boil the eggs for 5 minutes. Drain and leave to cool. Peel the lemon with a vegetable peeler and squeeze the juice. Add the lemon peel to the pan and simmer for a further 5–10 minutes, or until the beetroot is tender. Remove the lemon peel and discard. Pour the mixture into a food-processor, add the sugar, salt, lemon juice and herbs and blitz until smooth.

Wearing rubber gloves (because the potatoes will be hot) peel the potatoes, cut the flesh into small chunks and set aside. Peel the eggs, roughly chop and set aside. Toast the caraway seeds in a dry pan until they start to release their aroma, and set aside.

To serve, place a few chunks of hot potato in the bottom of each soup bowl. Sprinkle over some chopped egg and then ladle in the soup around the centre of the ingredients. Add a spoonful of soured cream in the centre and sprinkle over the toasted caraway seeds.

Variation
For a thicker soup, process the cooked potato with the beetroot soup and omit the sugar and lemon juice.

Meat Borscht

Compared to traditional Jewish borscht recipes, this is a rather souped up version (if you'll pardon the pun). Traditionally the main ingredients would have just included large amounts of beetroot, cabbage and potatoes with perhaps a bone for flavour. This version provides a more luxurious Russian emphasis with a piece of meat cooked in the liquid which can be served later as a delicious second course or for another meal.

Serves 8–10

6 large beetroot, peeled and roughly chopped
1 large onion, finely chopped
3 garlic cloves, peeled, green centre removed and finely chopped
3 celery stalks, trimmed and roughly chopped
1kg beef brisket, whole
1kg beef bones
1 lemon
2 tablespoons raisins
25g fresh flat-leaf parsley, finely chopped
25g fresh dill, finely chopped
1 teaspoon caraway seeds, toasted in a dry frying pan to release their aroma
2 organic free-range eggs

Place the beetroot in a large pan with the onion, garlic, celery, beef and beef bones. Pour over 3.6 litres water and bring to the boil. Skim off any scum that rises to the surface. Turn down the heat and simmer gently for about 2 hours.

Take out the beef brisket with a slotted spoon and set aside on a plate. Peel the lemon with a vegetable peeler and squeeze the juice. Add the lemon peel to the pan with the lemon juice, raisins, herbs and caraway seeds. Bring back to the boil and simmer for 5 minutes, stirring. Turn off the heat and discard the lemon peel and bones.

Break the eggs into a small bowl, whisk in a ladleful of the soup and then tip the mixture back into the pan, whisking all the time.

Cut the cooked brisket into bite-sized pieces and place some in the base of each soup bowl. (If it looks like there is too much for one meal, save some to have another day. Serve cold with a piece of potato kugel, salad and chraine (see page 228). Ladle the soup over the meat and accompany with dark rye bread and pickled cucumbers.

TEMPTING SOUPY EXTRAS

In Jewish eyes, unless a soup is really thick it is considered to be rather insubstantial. This is why thin soups and broths are often extended with noodles, dumplings or other accompaniments. A carefully made broth provides a wonderful vehicle for all sorts of magical delicacies – from knaidlach (dumplings) and kreplach (ravioli) to farfel (tiny pasta shapes) and other treats. These delectable extras originated when balabosters (mothers/homemakers) needed to extend a scrap of meat or chicken in a soup to feed an entire family. Today, however, they are revered as a delicacy.

Soup Mandelen

Serves 6–8

210g plain flour
¾ teaspoon baking powder
1 teaspoon salt
6 grinds of black pepper
2 teaspoons sesame or poppy seeds
2 organic free-range eggs
1½ tablespoons olive oil

Preheat the oven to 190°C/gas mark 5 and line two baking sheets with baking parchment. Sift the flour and baking powder into a large mixing bowl and stir in the salt, pepper and seeds. Beat the eggs with the olive oil and combine with the flour to make a dough. (Alternatively, blitz everything together in a food-processor.) If the dough is too stiff to roll, add an extra egg yolk to soften the mixture.

Roll out the dough thinly and cut out small diamonds or squares, 1 x 1cm. Lay the shapes on the prepared baking sheets and bake in the oven for about 10–15 minutes until golden. Store in a jar or tin and use as required.

Farfel

Farfel, I suspect, is the Jewish equivalent of pasta or couscous. A basic egg dough is grated to make rice-sized grains, which are dried until ready for use.

Makes about 400g

280g plain flour
¼ teaspoon salt
3 medium organic free-range eggs, beaten

Place the flour and salt in the bowl of your food-processor, pour in the beaten eggs with the motor running and mix to a soft pliable dough. Cut the dough in half, and leave the halves on a floured board to dry.

To make the farfel, grate the dry dough on the coarse side of a grater and spread out on a floured baking sheet lined with parchment paper. Place the farfel in an airy space to dry, and then store in a plastic bag in the freezer until ready to use.

To cook the farfel, simply drop them into your broth and simmer for about 10 minutes.

Nockerl

Goodness, these bring back childhood memories – my mother's smiling face, a steaming soup rich with tender clouds of eggy dough, a snow-white Shabbat cloth laden with silver. Perfect!

Serves 4

2 medium organic free-range eggs
1 teaspoon salt
70g plain flour
½ teaspoon baking powder

Beat the eggs and salt in a measuring jug with 55ml water. Sift the flour and baking powder into a bowl. Make a well in the centre, pour in the egg mixture and mix to a smooth batter.

To cook the nockerl, drop teaspoons of the batter into your soup or a pan of salted water. Wait until they rise to the surface and serve immediately.

Knaidlach

Knaidlach are also known as matzo balls or matzoh kleis in America. They are called *knaidel* or *knaydel* in Yiddish, both of which mean dumpling. The name originates from the old Southern German word *knodel*, also meaning dumpling. They were created by mothers fighting dire poverty during the Diaspora and began as a crushed potato seasoned and stuffed with a little goose fat. And those dumplings still exist.

However, over the years they became known as the more popular dumpling made out of crushed matzos or matzo-meal combined with eggs, oil or schmaltz (chicken fat) and water and sometimes a little sugar, ginger or (for special occasions) a touch of ground almonds. So again this humble dumpling could extend the use of an egg and a little fat into a highly nutritious soup addition. Now they are possibly the most popular soupy extra.

A fascinating story quoted in *Jewish Cooking in America* is that matzo-ball soup was served at MGM studios in Hollywood every day – the recipe supplied by Louis B. Meyer's mother. Hollywood ran on knaidlach!

Makes 128 walnut-size balls – perfect for Passover Seder
Halve or quarter for small family portions

500g medium matzo meal
1½ teaspoons salt
freshly ground black pepper, to taste
2 teaspoons bouillon powder, dissolved in 650ml hot water
100ml olive oil
15g fresh flat-leaf parsley, finely chopped
a large pinch of dried thyme
3 medium organic free-range eggs

To make the dough, place the matzo meal in a large mixing bowl with the salt. Pour in the dissolved bouillon powder, add the oil and chopped herbs and beat well to combine. Leave the mixture to cool slightly. Break in the eggs, one at a time, and beat well after each addition.

Form into walnut-size balls and lay on a matzo meal-lined platter. When finished drop the balls into hot stock. After 5 minutes, they will rise to the top. Either serve immediately or open freeze raw, then place in a plastic bag for instant soup additions.

Variation

Super-fluffy Knaidlach

Some balabosters base their reputations on the fluffiness of their knaidlach. In this recipe, the eggs are separated and the whisked whites folded in separately to give a fluffier texture.

Makes about 45 walnut-sized balls

2 medium organic free-range eggs
175g medium matzo meal
50g ground almonds
pinch of ground ginger (optional)
100ml olive oil
15g fresh flat-leaf parsley, finely chopped (optional)
freshly ground salt and black pepper

Separate the eggs. Place the matzo meal in a large mixing bowl with the ground almonds and ginger (if using) and stir in the olive oil and the parsley. Pour in 300ml hot water and beat well with a wooden spoon. Leave to cool slightly, then beat in the egg yolks. Set aside to swell for approximately 20 minutes.

Meanwhile, place the egg whites in a bowl and whisk until stiff peaks form. Stir a spoonful of the egg whites into the knaidlach mixture to soften it. Now carefully fold in the rest. Season with more salt and pepper if necessary. To shape the knaidlach, form the mixture into walnut-sized balls and chill or freeze until needed. To cook the knaidlach, poach in hot stock until the lovely balls rise to the surface. This takes about 5 minutes for fresh ones, or 10 minutes from frozen – or as long as it takes to get Jewish people seated round a table!

KREPLACH

These meltingly soft dough triangles with delicious fillings are similar to Italian ravioli. They are traditionally served on the night before the fast of Yom Kippur (Kol Nidrei night), Simchat Torah and Purim.

There are many explanations as to how kreplach got their name. One explanation suggests it is formed from the three initials K for Kippur, R for Rabba and P for Purim, which together sound out the word 'krep'; 'lach' comes from the Yiddish meaning 'little'. Another explanation is that they are named after the German word 'krepp' meaning 'crêpe', due to the thinness of their pastry. Some say that G-d hid when he was performing the miracle of saving the Jews, which explains the filling 'hidden' beneath the dough, while many people say the triangular shape represents Haman's hat.

Kreplach ⓟ

In homage to Queen Esther, who became a vegetarian living in a non-kosher court, I have suggested a filling of mashed chickpeas spiced with chillies for kreplach with a twist. However, they are equally gorgeous filled with leftover cooked meat or chicken, minced finely, flavoured with herbs and a pinch of cinnamon or cardamom, with an egg to bind.

These freeze really well, so if you have a quiet afternoon you can always make them in advance. The baking powder adds a hint of lightness; the saffron emphasises the gloriously golden eggy colour.

Makes 32–36

For the dough
2 organic free-range eggs
1 tablespoon olive oil
a pinch of saffron strands, steeped in 1 tablespoon hot water
225g plain flour
a pinch of salt
a pinch of baking powder

For the filling
1 x 235g tin chickpeas in water
1 heaped teaspoon tchina (oriental sesame paste) or tahini
½ teaspoon dried chopped chillies
1 teaspoon garam masala
¼ teaspoon ground turmeric
25g coriander, chopped
1 teaspoon ground paprika
freshly ground salt and black pepper

Beat the eggs with the oil in a measuring jug and strain in the soaking liquid from the saffron. Place the flour in the bowl of a food-processor with the salt and baking powder. Pour in the beaten egg mixture and mix to a soft, pliable dough. If the mixture is very sticky, add a little extra flour. Process the dough for about 5 minutes (or tip it out onto a work surface and knead well). Place the dough in a plastic bag and chill in the fridge for about 30 minutes.

To make the filling, place all the ingredients, including a little of the liquid from the chickpeas, in a food-processor and blitz to a smooth or coarse paste, depending on your preference. Season to taste with salt and pepper. Remove the dough from the fridge and roll out very thinly on a floured work surface. Cut into squares, 9 x 9cm. Place half a teaspoon of the filling in the centre of each square, wet the edges with a pastry brush and fold in half diagonally to form a triangle. Pinch around the filling to seal and prevent it leaking out during cooking.

You can either freeze the kreplach at this point or cook them immediately. Open freeze in a raw state on a floured baking sheet, lined with parchment paper. When frozen solid, pack into polythene bags or plastic boxes for later use. To cook the kreplach, bring a large pan of boiling stock or soup to the boil, drop in the kreplach and simmer for 5–7 minutes. Serve.

3: Fish

Jewish people have enjoyed fish since biblical times. Originally it was fried, dried in the sun or salted. By the Middle Ages, Jewish women were renowned for their ability to cure fish, creating a cottage industry. And soon fish became a symbolic part of a festive meal, representing fertility (due to the number of eggs and offspring fish produce). Jacob blessed his children saying that they should multiply like the fish in the sea. The rabbis who wrote the Mishnah (the written Torah) decreed that it would be beneficial for Jews to eat fish at each Shabbat meal, and so followed the saying: 'Without fish… there is no Sabbath'. Fish is hugely helpful to orthodox cooks who cannot cook on the Sabbath, since it can be offered hot or cold, with a dairy or before a meat meal.

Of course, today Jews are conscious of the problems of maritime conservation and these recipes reflect our concern.

'This you may eat from everything that is in the water, everything that has fins and scales… those you may eat.' LEVITICUS 11:9.

Soused Herrings (P)

These were once considered a poor man's meal, but when they are served with salad and crusty bread or a few tiny new-season potatoes, herrings make an elegant lunch or supper. Look for extremely fresh fish – they should have bright eyes and bright red gills (situated underneath the cavity just past the eye). Make sure there is no slime or scent of ammonia, just a lovely smell of the sea. Get your fishmonger to fillet the fish for you, although you may still have to remove some of the smaller bones – best done with an old pair of tweezers.

Serves 4–6

3 fat herrings, cleaned and filleted with all
  the bones removed
1 large red onion, thinly sliced
2 bay leaves
10 peppercorns
2 teaspoons yellow or black mustard seeds
6 tablespoons fairtrade soft brown sugar
200ml cider vinegar or red wine vinegar
50g sultanas (optional)

Lay the herring fillets in an oven-to-table dish, overlapping them slightly if necessary, and scatter over the onions. (I use a glass dish because it is easier to wash!) Alternatively, roll the herrings into little rounds, placing a few slices of onion inside the parcels. Combine the remaining ingredients with 6 tablespoons of water in a jug or similar and pour over the fish. Bake in the oven for about 20 minutes, or until the fish and onions are tender. Remove from the oven, set aside to cool and then chill in the fridge until needed.

Soused herrings can be stored in the fridge for up to 6 days.

Herrings in Soured Cream or Greek Yogurt (M)

Serves 4–6

4 pickled herrings from a jar
1 large eating apple (such as 'Jonagold', which is sweet and
  sharp and keeps its shape well)
150ml soured cream or Greek yogurt (equally rich and
  super healthy)
25g fresh flat-leaf parsley, finely chopped
25g fresh dill, finely chopped (optional)

For the cucumber salad
½ cucumber
freshly ground salt and black pepper

To garnish
a handful of black olives
a sprinkling of paprika (optional)

First prepare the cucumber salad. Remove the skin from the cucumber and cut the flesh into long ribbons using a vegetable peeler. Place the cucumber ribbons in a bowl, season with salt and pepper and set aside to draw out some of the water.

Cut the herrings into bite-sized pieces and place in a bowl. Grate in the apple, keeping the skin on for added colour, and stir in the soured cream or yogurt and herbs.

To serve, drain the cucumber and place a little pile on each serving plate. Add a spoonful of the herring mixture, garnish with a few black olives and finish with a dusting of paprika.

Salmon Rissoles

Ⓟ (with optional milky sauce)

My mother made the best salmon rissoles ever! It was the 1950s, money was tight – she needed to stretch a few meals out of a couple of tins of salmon. I watched her, my eyes barely reaching the Formica top, as she dropped perfect shapes into the foaming oil and then piled them up in a delicious heap on a china platter decorated with lemon crescents and parsley. Forty years on, the soul of the recipe lives on. Those rissoles, though grilled today for better health, are still arranged on that china platter and evoke all those lovely childhood moments.

This new healthier version has become one of my grandchildren's favourite in-from-school teas. The rissoles freeze well and make a delicious lunch or starter for a dinner party. Serve them with a watercress salad, dressed with a *milchig* dill and caper sauce mixed with fromage frais. To reheat, simply pop in the microwave or oven until piping hot.

Makes 24 rissoles

3 x 180g tins pink salmon (skinless and boneless)
3 x 180g tins red salmon (skinless and boneless)
plenty of freshly ground black pepper
6 organic free-range eggs
25g fresh flat-leaf parsley, roughly chopped
a few tips of fresh thyme
120ml good-quality light olive oil
150g medium matzo meal, plus extra for coating

Open the tins of salmon and tip the contents, along with any liquid, into a large mixing bowl. Season with about 12 grinds of black pepper (there is no need to add salt because the fish will be salty already).

Separate the eggs and add the yolks to the fish mixture. Place the whites in a food-processor with the parsley and thyme and blitz until the herbs are finely chopped and the eggs are fluffy. (If you don't have a food-processor, simply whisk the egg whites until stiff peaks form and fold in the finely chopped herbs.)

Add the oil to the fish mixture and mix thoroughly with a fork so there are no large chunks of fish. Add the egg whites and matzo meal and fold in carefully, keeping the mixture as light as possible. Set aside for 10 minutes to allow the matzo to swell. Meanwhile, sprinkle some matzo meal on a large platter ready for coating. Preheat your grill to moderate.

With wet hands form the mixture into 24 golfball-size balls and flatten them slightly with the palm of your hand to create a patty. Roll the rissoles in the matzo meal to coat and arrange on a grill tray. Grill for 5–7 minutes on each side until golden brown; watch that they do not burn.

Serve with a grated carrot and beetroot salad and chunks of really good granary bread or new potatoes.

Coulibiac of Smoked and Fresh Salmon ⓜ

This glorious Russian recipe with its elegant puff pastry fish shape makes a wonderful centrepiece for a winter party.

Serves 8–10

200g responsibly sourced fresh salmon slices
350g responsibly sourced hot smoked salmon fillets
juice and grated zest of ½ lemon
1 tablespoon butter
2 organic free-range eggs
2 large spring onions, finely chopped
1 tablespoon vegetable oil
450g wild or chestnut mushrooms, finely chopped
100g cooked rice of your choice
75g frozen peas – not strictly traditional but they look pretty!
25g fresh flat-leaf parsley, finely chopped
15g fresh dill, finely chopped
freshly ground salt and black pepper
2 x 425g packs ready-rolled puff pastry

Preheat the oven to 180°C/gas mark 4. Spread a large sheet of foil on your work surface. Cut the fresh salmon into large chunks and place on the foil. Add the hot smoked salmon, squeeze over the lemon juice and add the butter. Wrap up the fish to form a little parcel and lift onto a baking sheet. Bake in the oven for 15 minutes, and then set aside to cool.

Meanwhile, hard boil the eggs for 10 minutes; drain, cool and roughly chop.

In a large frying pan, gently fry the spring onion in the vegetable oil until soft. Add the mushrooms and cook until lightly coloured. Add the rice, peas, lemon zest and herbs and stir well so that everything is combined. Season with plenty of salt and pepper.

Turn up the oven to 220°C/gas mark 7. Roll out one pack of pastry to fit a baking sheet, 21 x 31cm. Cut the pastry into a large fish shape and carefully lift it onto a baking sheet. Pile half of the cooked salmon mixture on top, leaving a border all around the edges. Heap the rice and mushroom mixture on top of the fish and scatter over the chopped eggs. Top with the remaining fish.

Using a pastry brush, wet the edges of the pastry with water. Roll out the remaining block of pastry and carefully lay it over the fish. Press down carefully around the edges to seal, and then decorate with scales using the pastry trimmings. Chill in the fridge for 30 minutes. Beat the remaining egg with a pinch of salt to form an egg wash and brush over the pastry. Bake in the oven for about 30 minutes until golden brown. (If the pastry is browning too quickly, turn down the oven once the pastry has puffed up.) Serve and enjoy.

Whole Poached Salmon with Lemon Sauce (P)

This dish would have traditionally been made with halibut. However, as this fish is now endangered I have substituted salmon – although you can use any sustainably sourced firm-fleshed fish.

Serves 6–8

For the salmon
1 large onion, sliced
3 carrots (about 240g), peeled and roughly chopped
3 celery sticks, trimmed and roughly chopped
peel of 1 lemon (removed with a vegetable peeler)
a few sprigs of fresh thyme
1 bay leaf
1 vegetable stock cube
2 teaspoons salt
plenty of black pepper
1 x 1.5kg whole salmon (gutted, cleaned and scales removed – you can ask the fishmonger to do this)

For the sauce
4 organic free-range egg yolks
3–4 teaspoons fairtrade golden caster sugar
2 teaspoons salt
3 tablespoons cornflour
3–4 tablespoons lemon juice
25g fresh flat-leaf parsley, finely chopped

To prepare the poaching liquid, place the onion, carrots, celery, lemon peel and herbs in a large, wide pan. Dissolve the stock cube in 900ml water, add to the pan and bring to the boil. Season with the salt and about 20 grinds of black pepper. Turn down the heat and simmer for about 20 minutes, or until the vegetables are tender.

Carefully lower the salmon into the hot liquid, cover the pan with a lid and simmer very gently for 10 minutes. Switch off the heat and set aside to cool, if possible in the liquid. Once the salmon is cold, carefully remove it from the pan with two fish slices and place it on a large serving platter. (Reserve the cooking liquid for the sauce.) Carefully remove the skin from the fish.

To make the sauce, strain the cooking liquid through a nylon sieve into a clean pan. Place the egg yolks in a heatproof bowl and set over a pan of gently simmering water. Add the sugar and salt and whisk to combine. In a small bowl, mix the cornflour with the lemon juice. Pour the mixture into the egg yolks and add a ladleful of the cold poaching liquid, whisking all the time. Keep whisking as the mixture thickens to form a creamy sauce. If necessary, add a little more stock to achieve a coating consistency. Stir in the chopped parsley and spoon into a jug. Taste and season with salt and pepper, if necessary. Serve alongside the poached fish. Enjoy.

Smoking Your Own Salmon

How exciting and challenging to hot-smoke your own salmon! All you need is a wok and a little patience, and delectable smoked fish will be yours. The secret is to have a perfect seal between wok and lid.
Serves 2 as a main meal, or 3–4 as a starter with salad

500g fresh salmon or trout fillet (skin on)
olive oil, to brush
black pepper

For the smoking mixture
6 Earl Grey tea bags
50g brown sugar
50g uncooked rice
a sprig of fresh rosemary or thyme (optional)

Line a wok with a large piece of tin foil. Place the tea bags, brown sugar, rice and herbs in the base and sit a cooling rack or similar on top, making sure it fits fully inside the wok. Smear the fish all over with olive oil and season with black pepper. Place the fish on the rack, skin-side down. Bring the foil over the fish, leaving it loosely covered, and put on the lid.

Set the wok over a very low heat for about 10 minutes – a sneaking peek will reveal a waft of smoke. Remove the pan from the heat, keeping the lid on, and set aside for 20 minutes (somewhere far away from the smoke alarm) to allow the smoke to penetrate the fish. When you remove the lid, you should have delicious home-smoked salmon. Serve hot or cold.

Variation
Substitute with well-boned herring or mackerel fillets. For a spicy flavour, smear the fish with chilli oil or a little dukkah spice mix.

Lemon Spiced Gravlax

Curing your own fish is rewarding and economical. It's not difficult and you'll be delighted with the results.
Serves 8 generously

1kg fillet of salmon or trout (skin on)
1 teaspoon caraway seeds
1 teaspoon dill seeds
1 teaspoon fennel seeds
1 tablespoon limoncello
190g granulated sugar
160g salt
1 teaspoon coarse black pepper
50g fennel, finely sliced
peel of 1 lemon, removed with a vegetable peeler

Check the fish for bones and debone if necessary with tweezers. Rinse well to remove any remaining fish scales, and then cut lengthways through the middle to give you two matching halves. To make the curing mixture, grind the seeds with the limoncello in a mortar and pestle. Tip them into a bowl and add the sugar, salt and pepper.

Rub the salmon fillets all over with the curing mixture. Lay a large piece of clingfilm on your work surface, place one of the fillets on top and scatter over the fennel slices. Add the lemon peel. Place the remaining fillet on top and wrap up tightly in the clingfilm. Place in a glass dish. Put a lid or plate on top of the fish and weigh it down with tins or stones. Transfer the dish to the fridge and chill for 24 hours.

The next day, open up the clingfilm and baste the fish all over with the salty liquid that has collected in the bottom of the dish. Turn the fish over, rewrap and weight again. Repeat this process for 3–7 days.

To serve, scrape off the excess curing mixture and cut the fish into thin slices. Accompany with rye bread or pumpernickel flatbread and a few fresh radishes. This freezes well, sliced or whole.

Sephardi Hot Spiced Fish ⓟ

I watched this recipe lovingly prepared in a warm Fez kitchen. It explodes with flavour, showing the Sephardis' creativity in combining fruit, vegetables and spices to enhance the flavour of the fish.

Ask your fishmonger to prepare the fish for you by gutting it, scraping off all the scales and removing the large backbone. Removing the head is optional.

Serves 4–6

For the fish
1 red pepper, roughly chopped (seeds and membrane removed)
1 yellow pepper, roughly chopped (seeds and membrane removed)
1 large onion, roughly chopped
2 large plump fennel bulbs, roughly chopped
1 lemon, roughly chopped
1 small orange, roughly chopped
2 tomatoes, roughly chopped
2 bay leaves
2 cinnamon sticks
1 x 1.5kg whole fish, such as line-caught sea bass or bream
1 preserved lemon, finely chopped
120ml vegetable stock or white wine

For the Chermoula rub and filling
100g fresh flat-leaf parsley, finely chopped
100g fresh coriander, finely chopped
3 garlic cloves, peeled and finely crushed
2 teaspoons salt
1 teaspoon freshly ground black pepper
2 teaspoons paprika
¼ teaspoon cayenne pepper
1½ teaspoons ground cumin
a pinch of saffron strands
juice of ½ lemon
85ml olive oil
60ml vegetable oil

Preheat the oven to 180°C/gas mark 4. Combine the vegetables and fruit in a large ovenproof dish or roasting tin lined with foil. Add the bay leaves and cinnamon and lay the fish on top. Slash both sides of the fish with a sharp knife ready for the marinade.

Combine the ingredients for the Chermoula rub in a large bowl and mix well together. Divide the mixture into two. Add the finely chopped preserved lemon to one bowl and mix well. Using your hands, stuff this mixture into the cavity of the fish.

Take the second half of the mixture and spread it over the fish, rubbing it into the slits with your fingers. Pour over the vegetable stock or wine, cover with foil and bake in the oven for about 30–40 minutes or until the fish flakes easily when poked with a fork.

Bream in Sweet and Sour Sauce ⓟ

This recipe reaches back into the annals of Ashkenazi cookery and is particularly suitable for the Passover as the sauce is made without flour. The toasted pine nuts balance the sweetness of the raisins, while the addition of poached sliced fennel and a little chilli brings a modern twist to an old favourite.

You can ask the fishmonger to prepare the fish for you by gutting it, scraping off all the scales and removing the backbone.

Serves 4–6

For the bream
1 fennel bulb, thinly sliced
2 garlic cloves, finely chopped
2 celery sticks, thinly sliced
2 large onions, thinly sliced
2 bay leaves
a pinch of dried thyme
1 teaspoon chilli flakes (optional)
peel of 1 lemon, removed with a vegetable peeler
900ml light vegetable stock
freshly ground salt and black pepper
1 x 1–1.5kg whole bream or seabass (cleaned and gutted)

For the sauce
1 tablespoon caster sugar
1 tablespoon potato flour
juice of 1 lemon
2 tablespoons raisins
100g pine nuts or whole almonds, toasted in a dry frying pan until golden
2 spring onions, finely chopped
freshly ground salt and black pepper

To make the poaching liquid, place the fennel, garlic, celery, onion, herbs, chilli and lemon peel in a large pan. Pour over the stock and season with salt and pepper. Bring to the boil and simmer until the vegetables are tender – about 15–20 minutes.

You can either poach the fish whole or cut it into individual portions, which is easier and quicker. Turn the heat down low and poach the fish very gently until it is tender – about 15 minutes for a whole fish. Carefully lift out the fish with two fish slices and place on a large serving platter. Remove the vegetables with a slotted spoon and arrange them on the platter with the fish. Cover the dish with foil to keep everything warm while you make the sauce. Measure 450ml poaching liquid into a jug.

To make the sauce, place the sugar in a heavy-based pan over a gentle heat. Wait for the sugar to melt and then watch as it turns a light golden brown colour. Meanwhile, combine the potato flour with the lemon juice in a small bowl. Once the sugar has turned a nice caramel colour, quickly pour in the reserved fish stock and lemon mixture, whisking to combine. Stir in the raisins, pine nuts and spring onions. Bring to the boil and simmer for 10 minutes. Season to taste. To serve, pour the sauce over the fish and enjoy hot or cold.

Baked Sea Bass Stuffed with Olives and Herbs ⓟ

Orthodox families like to place the fish head facing the head of the household during the Rosh Hashanah (New Year) meal. As it is written in the bible: *'May we be as the head and not the tail'*, Deuteronomy 28:13.

This elegant dish is equally good served hot or cold. Ask your fishmonger to prepare the fish for you by gutting it, scraping off all the scales and removing the large backbone. Removing the head is optional.

Serves 8

1 x 1.5–2kg whole sea bass
1 lemon, cut into slices
olive oil, for drizzling

For the herb stuffing
1 large onion, finely chopped
1 tablespoon olive oil
25g fresh flat-leaf parsley
25g fresh dill
25g capers
1 organic free-range egg
50g pitted olives
100g fresh breadcrumbs
juice and grated zest of 1 lemon or lime
freshly ground salt and black pepper

Preheat the oven to 200°C/gas mark 6. To make the stuffing, gently fry the onion in the olive oil until tender and just starting to colour. Meanwhile, place the herbs, capers and egg in a food-processor and blitz until smooth. Scrape into a mixing bowl. Chop or pulse the olives and tip into the bowl with the herb mixture. Add the breadcrumbs, fried onions, lemon zest and juice and some salt and pepper. Mix well together.

Fill the cavity of the fish with the stuffing. Line a large baking sheet with a double layer of foil and arrange the lemon slices down the centre. Place the stuffed fish on top and drizzle with olive oil. Wrap up the fish to form a tight parcel and bake in the oven for 5 minutes. Now turn down the temperature to 170°C/gas mark 3 and bake for a further 30–35 minutes, or until the fish is tender and flakes when you poke it with a fork. Remove the fish from the oven, take off the foil and carefully scrape away the skin. Arrange on a serving dish and serve with hot new potatoes and a watercress salad.

Variations
Substitute 3–4 tablespoons white wine instead of the lemon juice.

For an oriental flavour, omit the olives, capers and dill and replace with a dash of soy sauce, a teaspoon of grated fresh ginger and plenty of chopped coriander.

Gefilte Fish (Fish Balls) (P)

Traditionally, balabosters faced with poverty would stuff a whole fish (usually a carp) with forcemeat or fish stuffing to extend it to feed a large number of people. However, today the stuffing has become a popular dish in its own right.

No Jewish function, especially a Kiddush in the synagogue, a wedding or family celebration called Simcha, would be complete without miniature fried gefilte fish served on cocktail sticks. They're often accompanied by small pieces of pickled herring on toast, olives and various types of crisps and nuts.

The larger size of 'chopped fried' or 'chopped and boiled', as gefilte fish are affectionately called, are served as a starter or light meal with salad, or after the Sabbath, as they are ready-prepared and quick to dish. Both are served with Chraine (see page 228), the remainder of the Shabbat challah and salad.

This is an unusual version of gefilte fish in that it contains a high proportion of cooked carrot. This lends a healthy sweetness to the fish balls and extra flavour. In Poland, gefilte fish is traditionally sweetened with sugar, while Jews who descended from Lithuanian immigrants (Litvak Jews) still prefer theirs unsweetened. Many people add a few grams of ground almonds to the mixture to make the fish balls richer in flavour, but these are prepared without them.

Makes approximately 40 balls

For the fish mixture
2 large organic free-range eggs
2 large carrots, boiled until tender (or 1 x 300g tin of carrots, drained)
25g fresh flat-leaf parsley
50ml olive oil
1kg mixed fish, such as farmed cod or more sustainable pollock, haddock and bream, filleted and minced (ask your fishmonger to mince it for you)
freshly ground salt and black pepper
about 150g medium matzo meal, to bind

For the poaching liquid
some fish bones (optional)
1 large onion, quartered
2 large carrots, peeled and cut into 1cm rings
2 celery sticks, roughly chopped
600ml vegetable stock

Place the poaching ingredients in a large pan and simmer for about 20 minutes, until the vegetables are tender. (If you remembered to ask your fishmonger for the bones, put them in the pan as well but take care to simmer the stock very gently, not boil it, or it will become grey.) Strain the liquid through a nylon sieve into a clean pan ready to poach the gefilte fish. Remove the carrots from the stock and set aside to be used as decoration on top of each piece of fish (as they signify coins and are a way of wishing prosperity).

To make the fish mixture, first separate the eggs. Then, in a large mixing bowl, add the cooked or tinned carrots, along with the egg yolks, parsley, olive oil, matzo meal and salt and pepper. Tip in the minced fish and then gently fold in the egg whites, making sure not to lose the fluffiness of the mixture. The mixture will seem on the soft side, but do avoid adding any more matzo meal as this will harden the fish. Set the mixture aside for 5–10 minutes to allow the matzo meal to swell. Shape the mixture into 40 golfball-sized balls, adding a little more matzo meal at this stage if the mixture still seems too soft.

To cook the gefilte fish, bring the strained stock back to the boil. Lower the fish balls into the gently bubbling stock and simmer for 10–12 minutes. Alternatively, pour the stock into a deep glass microwaveable bowl, add the fish balls and cook in the microwave on high for 5–7 minutes.

You can either eat the fish balls straight away (the healthiest choice!) or dust them in matzo meal (medium works best), flatten them slightly and shallow-fry them until crisp – rather like a rissole. For a healthier alternative to frying, simply dust in matzo meal and set under the grill for 5–7 minutes on each side until golden.

Variation
To give this main meal an oriental twist, combine 1 tin of coconut milk in a bowl with 2 teaspoons chilli dipping sauce. Add 3 large spring onions, chopped on the diagonal, 1 thumb-size piece of peeled and grated fresh ginger, 1 stick of finely chopped lemongrass, the grated zest of 1 lime and 25g finely chopped fresh coriander. Salt to taste. Place the fish balls in an ovenproof dish, pour over the mixture, and bake in the oven at 180°C/gas mark 4 for 30 minutes. Serve with jasmine rice, steamed baby sweetcorn and mangetout peas.

4: Meat

For Jews, meat cookery through the ages has been shaped by two factors – the scarcity and expense of good-quality produce, and the limitations imposed by the laws of kashrut. Not only was it tough to afford the best cuts but, for the most part, the hind quarters of the animal could not be used. The use of blood is also banned (which means the concept of rare meat never really took off in the kosher world). A cuisine evolved around making the most of what could be used – these tended to be the cheaper, tougher parts of the animal which needed long, slow cooking (in the case of the Shabbat cholent, this could be up to 18 hours). The aim was to produce comforting, filling food at low cost. This style of food was never fashionable… until now, that is. The movement for slow food means that the very cooking methods disdained as old fashioned are now bang on trend. This is the perfect time to rediscover (and perhaps to tweak) a few of the dishes that proved their worth over many a long Russian winter, and to add a few Sephardi flourishes to liven them up a bit.

Salt Beef

You can buy beef ready pickled, but it is simple to do yourself if you don't live near a supplier. Traditional salt beef recipes include saltpetre, but because the government has become a little twitchy about giving the public free access to ingredients that can be used to make explosives, this is no longer available. The salt beef will taste just as good without it, but it will not have that characteristic vivid red colour.

Serves 4–6

600g salt
300g caster sugar
1 teaspoon black peppercorns
8 allspice berries
4 bay leaves
1 x 2kg piece of beef brisket
1 whole garlic bulb

To make the brine, place the salt, sugar, pepper, allspice and bay leaves in a large saucepan. Pour in 3.5 litres water and bring to the boil. Remove from the heat and set aside to cool.

Place the brisket in a large plastic container, pour over the brine to cover and pop the garlic on top. Fasten with a lid and place in the fridge for 7–14 days, depending on how cured you like your beef. You will need to turn the beef every day and keep it submerged – use tongs to ensure a minimum of bacteria is introduced.

After the required time in the fridge, remove the beef from the brine and wash it thoroughly to remove any excess salt. Your salt beef is now ready to cook.

Salt Beef with Knaidlach

Salt beef and knaidlach are both iconic Jewish dishes, but for some reason we never seem to put them together. Salt beef is paired with rye bread and knaidlach are reserved for chicken soup. However, they go together beautifully and make a wonderfully warming and comforting mid-winter meal.

Serves 4

1kg salt beef (see opposite)
1 carrot, peeled
1 onion, halved
1 celery stick, halved
2 bay leaves
10 peppercorns
a bunch of fresh flat-leaf parsley (including the stalks),
    plus extra to garnish

¼ quantity knaidlach (see page 61)

Place the brisket in a large saucepan and cover with water. Bring to the boil, and then turn down the heat to simmering point. Skim off any foam that has formed on the surface and add the carrot, onion, celery, bay leaves, peppercorns and parsley. Simmer over a low heat for about 3 hours until the meat is tender.

Meanwhile, make the knaidlach (see page 61) and shape into 16 golfball-sized balls.

Remove the meat, place on a carving board and cover with foil to keep warm. Remove and discard the vegetables, and then put the pan back on the heat. Drop the knaidlach balls into the bubbling liquid and cook for 15–20 minutes.

To serve, carve the salt beef thickly and place in the bottom of four serving bowls. Add the knaidlach and ladle over a few spoonfuls of the salt-beef broth. Garnish with fresh parsley.

Essig Fleisch
(Sweet and Sour Beef) Ⓕ

In this traditional Ashkenazi recipe (which translates rather prosaically as vinegar meat), the beef is slowly braised in stock, vinegar and sugar.
Serves 4

2 tablespoons vegetable oil
1kg braising steak, cut into large cubes
1 large onion, finely chopped
2 celery sticks, finely chopped
1 tablespoon plain flour
1 tablespoon tomato purée
100ml white wine vinegar
1½ tablespoons caster sugar
200ml chicken stock
freshly ground salt and black pepper

Heat 1 tablespoon oil in a large casserole over a high heat. Add the beef and sear it in the hot oil until brown on all sides – you may need to do this in batches. Remove the meat and set aside on a plate. Turn the heat down low, add a further tablespoon of oil and gently fry the onions and celery until soft but not coloured.

Put the beef back in the pan, increase the heat to medium-high and add the flour and tomato purée. Cook, stirring constantly, for a minute or two. Now add the vinegar and sugar and cook for a further minute, stirring. Pour in the chicken stock, season well with salt and pepper and bring to the boil. Turn the heat down low, put on a lid and simmer gently for about 2 hours. Serve with rice or mashed potatoes.

Liver Schnitzel
with Red Wine Sauce Ⓕ

It is best to use mild-tasting liver such as lamb's liver or, if you have recently had a pay rise, calves' liver. The flour and matzo meal give a beautifully crunchy bite, which contrasts with the soft texture of the liver. The liver should be koshered before frying.
Serves 2

For the schnitzel
150g plain flour
150g fine matzo meal
200g lamb's liver or calves' liver, koshered by holding it over a flame (see method on page 37)
2–3 tablespoons vegetable oil

For the sauce
1 onion, finely chopped
1 tablespoon vegetable oil
100ml red wine
a splash of port
100ml chicken stock
freshly ground salt and black pepper

To make the sauce, gently fry the onion in the oil until soft but not coloured. Turn up the heat, add the red wine and port and boil rapidly for 2–3 minutes to burn off the alcohol. Pour in the chicken stock and boil rapidly to reduce the volume by half. Season to taste, remove from the heat and set aside.

To make the schnitzels, tip the flour and matzo meal onto two separate plates. Dip the liver first into the flour and then into the matzo meal and coat on both sides. Season with salt and pepper.

In a large, heavy-based frying pan, heat 1 tablespoon oil over a moderate heat. Put in the livers and fry for 1–2 minutes on each side until golden brown – you might have to do this in batches. Transfer to serving plates and accompany with the red wine sauce.

Oxtail Cholent Ⓕ

Cholent, the Shabbat stew baked overnight on Friday to be eaten on Saturday at lunchtime, has a reputation for being comforting but bland. This Ashkenazi-meets-Sephardi version is spiked with Moroccan spices and chilli, and manages to be comforting and exciting all at the same time. We use oxtail, which is almost uniquely suited to this style of slow cooking, but you could use any cut of beef that requires slow cooking.

Serves 4

2 tablespoons vegetable oil
1½ kg oxtail, cut into pieces
100g pearl barley
1 teaspoon dried chilli flakes
1 teaspoon ground cumin
1 teaspoon ground coriander
1 cinnamon stick
1 star anise
700ml chicken stock
a pinch of saffron strands, steeped in a little hot water
4 garlic cloves, peeled and crushed
4 large potatoes, peeled and cut in half
freshly ground salt and black pepper
100g tinned chickpeas (drained weight)
a handful of fresh coriander, finely chopped, to garnish
extra virgin olive oil, to drizzle

Preheat the oven to 130°C/gas mark 1. Heat the oil in a large casserole, put in the oxtail pieces and sear until browned all over. Add the pearl barley, chilli and spices and stir briefly to release their aroma. Pour in the stock and add the saffron water and garlic.

Slip the potatoes in amongst the oxtail and season well. Bring to the boil. Cover the casserole with foil and then put on the lid. Bake in the oven for 4 hours. Just before you are about to serve, take off the lid and tip in the chickpeas. Return to the oven for a further 15 minutes. To serve, scatter with chopped coriander and drizzle with extra virgin olive oil.

Meatballs in Tomato Sauce (F)

Gedempte (slow-cooked) meatballs are an essential part of the Ashkenazi experience, using as they do the cheap cuts of meat to make a filling meal. I've given two meatball recipes here – a traditional one and an easy variation for when there is just not enough time to start grating onion and beating egg.

Serves 4

For traditional meatballs
800g minced beef
150g fine matzo meal
1 organic free-range egg, beaten
1 onion, coarsely grated
freshly ground salt and black pepper

For the tomato sauce
1 onion, finely chopped
2 garlic cloves, peeled and finely chopped
1 tablespoon olive oil
1 x 400g tin chopped tomatoes
1 teaspoon ground allspice
1 teaspoon ground cinnamon
freshly ground salt and black pepper

First make the tomato sauce. In a large casserole, gently fry the onion and garlic in the oil until soft but not coloured. Add the tomatoes, spices and seasoning and simmer gently for 10–15 minutes, adding a little water to thin the sauce if necessary.

To make the meatballs, combine all the ingredients in a large bowl and mix thoroughly with your hands. Season well and roll into golfball-sized balls.

Once the tomato sauce is ready, drop in the meatballs, cover with a lid and simmer gently for 30 minutes until the meatballs are cooked. Serve with rice or couscous.

Variation
For quick meatballs, combine 400g minced beef with 400g beef or chicken sausagemeat (you will have to remove the skins first). Season lightly, remembering the sausagemeat will already be seasoned, and roll into golfball-sized balls. Cook as above.

Roast Shoulder of Lamb with Kasha Stuffing ⒡

Kasha is roasted buckwheat, also known as 'groats'. While it doesn't have a glamorous reputation, it does have a wonderful nutty flavour that is offset here with mushrooms and sweet onion. One of the great things about this stuffing is it absorbs all the lamby juices through the slow roasting. You'll need a really good carving knife as the lamb will be meltingly soft, but with a three-hour cooking time you will have plenty of time to get sharpening.

Serves 6–8

1 mug (about 200g) buckwheat
1 large onion, finely chopped
100g button mushrooms, finely chopped
2 tablespoons vegetable oil
a sprig of fresh thyme (leaves only), finely chopped
freshly ground salt and black pepper
1kg boned shoulder of lamb
100ml white wine

Preheat the oven to 150°C/gas mark 2. First make the stuffing. Place the buckwheat in a dry frying pan and toast over a medium-high heat until browned but not burnt. Tip the buckwheat into a saucepan, cover with 2 mugfuls of water (use the same mug you used to measure the buckwheat) and bring to the boil. Simmer for about 20 minutes or until the water has been absorbed.

Meanwhile, in a large frying pan, gently fry the onion and mushrooms in the oil until tender – about 10 minutes. Add the chopped thyme, stir in the cooked buckwheat and season well.

Open out the lamb on a flat surface and season it well on both sides. Spoon the stuffing in a line down the middle, roll into a cylinder and fasten with string at regular intervals. (If there is too much stuffing, pack it into an oiled loaf tin and roast it separately for 45 minutes.) Place the stuffed lamb in a roasting tin, cover with foil and bake in the oven for 2 hours.

Remove the lamb from the oven and increase the temperature to 180°C/gas mark 4. Take off the foil and drain off any excess fat. Add half a glass of water to the pan and return it to the oven for a further hour.

Remove the lamb from the oven and carefully transfer the meat to a serving dish. To make the gravy, place the roasting tin on the hob, add the white wine and boil rapidly to reduce it by half. Season if necessary.

Serve the lamb with roast or mashed potatoes and gravy. For that authentic shtetl touch, accompany with some warmed sauerkraut generously seasoned with black pepper.

Pulled Lamb with Chraine (F)

It's about time someone tried to bring Jewish shtetl cuisine into the 21st century – and what better way than with this shredded lamb wrap? The Chinese have their duck pancakes, the Americans have barbecued meat sandwiches, so why shouldn't we join the party? The only non-Ashkenazi thing about this sandwich is the wrap itself, but if you feel strongly you could always try it in a bagel.

Serves 8

1kg shoulder of lamb
plenty of freshly ground salt and black pepper
1 teaspoon ground caraway seeds
8 soft tortilla wraps
2 tablespoons Chraine (see page 228)
1 x 400ml jar of sauerkraut
4 tomatoes, sliced
1 cucumber, sliced

Preheat the oven to 150°C/gas mark 2. Rub salt generously over the lamb shoulder, sprinkle with the ground caraway seeds and season with pepper. Place in a roasting tray, cover the tray with foil and seal as tightly as possible. Bake in the oven for 3 hours.

Remove the lamb from the oven and discard the foil. Raise the temperature to 180°C/gas mark 4 and return the lamb to the oven for a further hour. When the lamb is ready, put it on a carving board and shred the meat from the bone (the best way is with two forks).

To serve, warm the wraps in a dry frying pan or (if you are feeling brave) over a gas flame. Smear with as much chraine as required, then add the sauerkraut and sliced tomato and cucumber. Top with some shredded lamb and roll up as tightly as possible. Now attempt to eat it without making a mess everywhere!

Variation
If you are not a fan of chraine, this recipe will go equally well 'Sephardi-style' with the Yemenite Zhug recipe on page 96.

Lamb Goulash

When the Jews emigrated from Hungary they brought their paprika-scented goulash with them. It has since become a standard Ashkenazi dish, almost always made with beef. However, the Hungarians have almost infinite variations, involving different kinds of meats including mutton or lamb. Goulash is often served with pasta. We have used potato gnocchi, which turns out to be a marriage made in heaven.

Serves 4

1 onion, finely chopped
2 garlic cloves, peeled and finely chopped
2 tablespoons vegetable oil
1kg boned shoulder of lamb, excess fat removed and diced into 2cm cubes
2 tablespoons paprika
1 teaspoon crushed caraway seeds
1 tablespoon tomato purée
4 roasted and peeled red peppers (you can roast your own if you wish, but jarred ones are fine)
freshly ground salt and black pepper
100ml white wine
400g potato gnocchi
a handful of fresh flat-leaf parsley, finely chopped

In a large casserole, gently fry the onions and garlic in 1 tablespoon oil until soft but not coloured.

Meanwhile, heat a large frying pan over a high heat with the remaining tablespoon of oil and sear the lamb until nicely brown on all sides. Remove the lamb with a slotted spoon and add to the casserole with the onions. Add the paprika, caraway seeds, tomato purée and roasted peppers. Season well and stir thoroughly to coat the meat in the tomato and spices. Pour in the white wine, bring to the boil and then turn down the heat very low. Cover with a lid and simmer gently for 2–3 hours. Preheat the oven to 150°C/gas mark 2.

Remove the lid, pour over enough boiling water to cover the lamb and bring to the boil. Put on the lid and bake in the oven for a further 2 hours.

When the cooking time is up, remove the casserole from the oven. Cook the gnocchi according to the packet instructions; drain and add to the goulash. Give everything a gentle stir and serve in large pasta bowls, garnished with chopped parsley.

Sweet Potato Tortilla with Wurst (F)

This is a modern take on that midweek standby, wurst and eggs. Wurst, otherwise known as kosher salami, is defiantly pink and rubbery. But it does go very nicely in a Spanish omelette.

Serves 4

1 onion, sliced
1–2 tablespoons vegetable oil
100g wurst, cut into small cubes
1 large sweet potato, peeled and cut into 3mm slices
1 green or red chilli, finely chopped
freshly ground salt and black pepper
4 large organic free-range eggs

In a large frying pan, gently fry the onion in the oil until soft and just starting to colour. Add the wurst and stir for a couple of minutes, then add the sweet potato. Add the chilli and seasoning and give everything a good stir. Cover with a lid, turn down the heat very low and cook gently for about 20 minutes until the sweet potato is soft.

Meanwhile, beat the eggs with some salt and pepper in a bowl. Once the onion and potato mixture is cooked, turn the heat up to medium and pour in the beaten eggs. As the eggs start to set, use a spatula to draw in the edges to the middle of the pan so that the runny egg collects at the sides. When no more runny egg is left, take the pan off the heat.

This is the tricky bit. Place a large plate over the pan, take a deep breath and invert the pan over the plate. If all goes well the omelette should be sitting on the plate. Now slide the omelette back into the pan, so the cooked side is on top. Put the omelette back on the heat for a minute or so to brown the base. (If this sounds too precarious an operation, simply leave the omelette in the pan and place it under a moderate grill to brown the top.)
To serve, cut the omelette into wedges and accompany with salad. Enjoy warm or cold.

5: Poultry

Poultry plays a huge part in Jewish tradition. Chicken dishes have become synonymous with the Friday night Shabbat dinner, which also serves to illustrate how poultry was traditionally used. The chicken, usually an old bird that had reached the end of a long career laying eggs, would be boiled long and slow to produce that iconic broth, Jewish chicken soup. The chicken, now edible after several hours in the pot, would then often be roasted and served as a main course. Every part of the chicken would be used, from the liver to the schmaltz (chicken fat), which was almost a currency in the shtetl. Inevitably, it was about calories and comfort. Yet when Jews sit down for Shabbat dinner around the world today, they still eat a soup made in pretty much the same way as in the 19th century. Jews took their love of poultry abroad with them, and now there are a huge number of ready-cooked poultry products – from Vienna sausages and smoked goose to that new and unlikely delicacy, turkey shawarma.

Chicken and Rice with Zhug (F)

This is the ultimate marriage of Ashkenazi and Sephardi cooking on a plate – poached chicken, rice cooked in chicken stock and a fiery sauce. Zhug is originally from Yemen, but the Israelis have adopted it as their national condiment.

Serves 4

For the chicken and rice
1.5kg chicken thighs and/or legs
1 carrot, peeled but left whole
1 onion, peeled and cut in half
1 celery stick
1 teaspoon ground turmeric
1 chicken stock cube
freshly ground salt and black pepper
1 mugful (about 200g) basmati rice

For the zhug
2 garlic cloves
1 teaspoon cardamom pods
½ teaspoon caraway seeds
1 teaspoon cumin seeds
1 teaspoon coriander seeds
1 large bunch of fresh coriander, roughly chopped
1 large bunch of fresh flat-leaf parsley, roughly chopped
1–2 green chillies (depending on how hot you want your sauce),
    finely chopped
juice of ½ lemon
1 tablespoon olive oil

Place the chicken in a large pot and add enough water to cover, plus 5cm. Bring to the boil, turn down the heat to a gentle simmer and skim off any scum that collects on the surface. Add the vegetables, turmeric and stock cube and season with salt and pepper. Simmer very gently for 1 hour, and then remove the chicken and set aside on a plate. Reserve the stock for later.

To make the zhug, blanch the garlic in boiling water for 5 minutes. Place the cardamom pods in a large pestle and mortar and crush. Discard the husks and grind the seeds. Add the other spices and grind thoroughly. Add the chopped herbs, chillies, peeled garlic and a pinch of salt and pound for a couple of minutes to a coarse paste. Finally put in the lemon juice and olive oil and mix to a thick, pouring consistency.

To make the rice, place one mugful of rice in a saucepan with 2 mugfuls of the reserved chicken stock. Bring to the boil on a high heat, and then turn down the heat to low and cover with a lid. Cook for 15 minutes until all the liquid has been absorbed and the rice is fluffy.

Meanwhile, skin the chicken and remove all the bones. To serve, spoon the rice onto plates, arrange the chicken on top and finish with a good dollop of zhug.

Chicken and Barley Risotto (F)

Chicken soup with barley is a Jewish classic, but by tweaking the cooking method slightly I have given it a trendy Italian makeover. It tastes wonderful and is thrifty too – pearl barley is a fraction of the price of risotto rice.

Serves 4

1 onion or 2 shallots, finely chopped
4 tablespoons olive oil
200g pearl barley
100ml white wine
800ml chicken stock
a sprig of fresh tarragon
freshly ground salt and black pepper
800g diced chicken thigh meat
150g mushrooms, roughly chopped
25ml extra virgin olive oil

In a large casserole, gently fry the onion in 2 tablespoons olive oil until soft but not coloured. Add the pearl barley and stir for a minute or so. Add the wine and bubble away until it has almost completely been absorbed by the barley. Pour in the chicken stock and bring to the boil. Add the tarragon, season with salt and pepper and simmer on a low heat with the lid on for about 50 minutes, or until the barley is tender and the liquid is absorbed.

Meanwhile, heat the remaining olive oil in a large frying pan over a medium-high heat. Add the diced chicken and mushrooms, season with salt and pepper and fry until the chicken is cooked through and all the juices from the mushrooms have evaporated.

Once the barley is tender, add the chicken and mushrooms to the casserole and stir well to combine. Simmer for a further 5 minutes to allow the flavours to amalgamate, then pour in the extra virgin olive oil and stir well. Spoon into serving bowls and accompany with a green salad and a large glass of white wine.

Tagliatelle Frinsidisi

This wonderful twist on Friday night roast chicken, Italian-style, is an adaptation of a traditional Roman Shabbat dish that appeared in Claudia Roden's *Book of Jewish Food*. My version is a beautiful combination of sweet and savoury.

Serves 8

1 medium chicken
3 tablespoons olive oil, plus extra for drizzling
1 lemon
freshly ground salt and black pepper
100g pine nuts
1 onion
50g dried apricots, finely chopped
50g raisins, soaked in a little hot water
a sprig of fresh rosemary, finely chopped
500g tagliatelle

Preheat the oven to 190°C/gas mark 5. Smear the chicken with olive oil and pop it in a roasting tray. Halve the lemon, insert into the cavity and season well inside and out with salt and pepper. Bake in the oven, breast-side down, for 45 minutes. Remove the chicken from the oven, turn it breast side up and return it to the oven for a further 45 minutes (1½ hours in total).

Meanwhile, toast the pine nuts in a dry pan until golden. In a separate, large frying pan, gently fry the onion in 2 tablespoons olive oil until golden brown. Stir in the apricots, raisins and rosemary and set aside.

Once the chicken is cooked, remove it from the oven and set aside until cool enough to handle. Strip the meat from the carcass, chop coarsely and add to the onion mixture with the cooking juices and pine nuts. Season to taste.

In a large pan, boil the tagliatelle according to the packet instructions until al dente. Drain and add to the chicken mixture, along with a couple of tablespoons of the cooking water. Remove the lemon from the chicken cavity, squeeze in the juice and mix thoroughly. Serve piled high in pasta bowls with a glass of Shabbat red wine.

P'tcha (F)

P'tcha, otherwise known as calves' foot jelly, is one of the most authentic and iconic dishes from the shtetl. However, the thought of eating calves' feet tends to put people off these days and, besides, you don't see too many calves' feet on the butcher's slab! But you can create a similar dish with chicken pieces, which makes a good alternative to chicken soup on a Friday night. Invite your granny round and watch her eyes mist over when you serve it.

Serves 4–6

1kg chicken pieces – legs and wings work best
1 carrot, peeled but left whole
1 celery stick, peeled but left whole
1 large onion, peeled and cut in half
1 chicken stock cube
2 organic free-range eggs
freshly ground salt and black pepper
4 tablespoons agar flakes
1 bunch of fresh flatleaf parsley, finely chopped
melba toast, to serve

Place the chicken pieces in a large saucepan and pour over about 1 litre water to cover. Bring to the boil, reduce the heat to a gentle simmer and skim off any scum from the surface. Add the vegetables, crumble in the stock cube and simmer for 1 hour. Meanwhile, hard boil the eggs; drain, cool and slice.

Remove the chicken pieces and discard the vegetables. Add the agar flakes to the pan, stir briefly and simmer for 5 minutes. Then remove the pan from the heat and set aside.

Arrange the sliced egg in the base of a large square dish. Remove the bones from the chicken pieces and cut the meat into cubes. Arrange the chicken in a layer over the egg and scatter over a thin layer of parsley. Pour over the chicken stock. Cover the dish with clingfilm and transfer to the fridge to set for a few hours (or overnight if possible).

Cut the p'tcha into cubes and serve with melba toast and an extra flourish of parsley.

Chicken Tagine

Until the middle of the 20th century there was a large Jewish community in Morocco and when they emigrated they took their tagines with them. This dish, flavoured with lemon and coriander and spiked with black olives, is a typical, easy-to-make casserole.
Serves 4

8 large chicken thighs
4 garlic cloves, peeled and crushed
juice and grated zest of 1 lemon
2 tablespoons olive oil
1 onion, finely chopped
1 teaspoon ground ginger
1 teaspoon ground coriander
a large pinch of saffron, steeped in a little hot water
freshly ground salt and black pepper
a large handful of kalamata olives
a handful of fresh coriander leaves, finely chopped

Place the chicken thighs in a bowl, add the crushed garlic and lemon zest and juice and leave to marinate for at least an hour (preferably overnight).

Heat the olive oil in a casserole over a high heat and fry the marinated chicken in batches until golden brown. Set aside. Reduce the heat to medium, add the onion and sauté for a couple of minutes. Put the chicken back in the pan, add the ground ginger, ground coriander and saffron and stir for a couple of minutes to release their aroma. Season with salt and pepper. Cover with boiling water from the kettle. Bring to the boil, turn down the heat low and cover with a lid. Simmer gently for 30 minutes until the chicken is cooked through.

To serve, stir in the olives and coriander. Accompany with couscous on the side.

Chicken and Wurst Pie

This dish is filling, cheap and child friendly – definitely worth the calories!
Serves 4

100g plain flour
freshly ground salt and black pepper
1kg chicken thighs, skinned, filleted and diced
2 tablespoons vegetable oil
1 onion, finely chopped
2 garlic cloves, peeled and finely chopped
100ml red wine
1 x 500g carton of passata
250g beef wurst, diced
1 teaspoon paprika
500g kosher (parve) puff pastry
1 organic free-range egg, beaten

Place the flour in a bowl with some salt and pepper, add the chicken meat and toss well to coat.

Heat 2 tablespoons vegetable oil in a large casserole, add the chicken and brown quickly over a medium-high heat. Remove from the pan and set aside. Add a further 1 tablespoon oil to the pan, turn down the heat and put in the onion and garlic. Fry gently for 5–10 minutes until soft but not coloured. Put the chicken back in the pan, turn up the heat and pour in the wine. Boil rapidly to evaporate the alcohol and reduce it slightly, and then add the passata, wurst, paprika and some salt and pepper. Place a lid on the pan and simmer gently over a low heat for 1 hour. Switch off the heat and set aside to cool completely.

Preheat the oven to 190°C/gas mark 5.

When the chicken mixture is cool, tip it into a pie dish. Roll out the puff pastry to cover the pie dish so it is about 5mm thick. Cut off any excess pastry, crimp the edges with a fork and brush all over with beaten egg. Cut a cross in the centre of the pie to allow the steam to escape.

Bake in the oven for about 35 minutes until the pastry is risen and golden brown. Serve immediately.

Turkey Schnitzel with Salsa Verde (F)

Who knew that the best accompaniment for classic schnitzel was salsa verde? The fresh, pungent herbs go fantastically well with the crunchy escalope. You can also team salsa verde with fried fish fillets, in which case you should add two chopped anchovy fillets to make the recipe more authentic. According to the laws of kashrut, fish cannot be served on the same plate as a meat dish.

Serves 2

For the schnitzel
2 x 200g turkey breast steaks
2 teaspoons Dijon mustard
freshly ground salt and black pepper
2 organic free-range eggs, beaten
250g medium matzo meal
vegetable oil, for shallow-frying

For the salsa verde
a handful of fresh basil
a handful of fresh mint
a handful of fresh flat-leaf parsley
1 garlic clove, peeled
1 teaspoon capers
2 tablespoons olive oil
a pinch of salt
juice of 1 lemon

To make the schnitzel, bat out the turkey steaks with a meat tenderiser, rolling pin or, if you've had a rough day, a fist. Spread a teaspoon of mustard on each breast and season with a little salt and pepper. Break the eggs into a dish and tip the matzo meal onto a plate. Coat the turkey breasts first in the beaten egg, and then in the matzo meal until coated on both sides.

To make the salsa verde, put all the ingredients in a blender or food-processor and blitz to a smooth paste. (If you don't have a food-processor, you can make it in the traditional way using a pestle and mortar. In which case, purée the garlic first with a little salt, then finely chop the herbs and add them with the capers. Once you have broken them down, add the lemon juice and olive oil.)

To cook the schnitzels, heat 1cm vegetable oil in a large frying pan over a high heat. Wait for it to get smoking hot, and then put in the turkey steaks. Fry for about 2 minutes on each side, or until golden brown on both sides and cooked through.

Serve with a dollop of salsa verde.

DIY Shawarma

Turkey shawarma, served with a wide array of sauces and salads, is a uniquely Israeli street dish that has begun to catch on in kosher restaurants around the world. Making your own couldn't be simpler. All you need is a giant rotisserie and a huge lump of meat, made with layers of turkey interspersed with lamb fat! Or you can try my cheat's version made with chicken thighs, which are more tender than turkey meat.

Serves 2

350g skinless chicken thigh fillets
1 teaspoon ground cumin
1 teaspoon ground coriander
freshly ground salt and pepper
4 tablespoons tahini paste
juice of 1 lemon
2 tablespoons zhug (see page 96)
2 pitta breads
½ cucumber, finely chopped
2 tomatoes, finely chopped
2 pickled gherkins, finely chopped

Preheat the grill to its highest setting. Place the chicken pieces in a bowl, sprinkle over the cumin, coriander and some salt and black pepper and carefully rub the spices into the flesh. Arrange on a grill tray and set under the grill for 5 minutes on each side, or until golden brown and cooked through.

Meanwhile, make the tahini dressing. Place the tahini in a bowl, add the lemon juice and mix to a smooth paste with a little water. At first, it will seem as if the lemon has curdled it, but if you keep on stirring it will end up the consistency of double cream. Season with salt to taste.

To assemble your shawarma, warm the pitta under the grill. Carve the chicken into thin strips (almost shredded) and stuff inside the pitta bread. Spoon some tahini dressing and zhug on top and add some chopped cucumber, tomato and gherkin. Finish with another squeeze of lemon.

Roast Duck
Polish Style ⓕ

This is roast duck Eastern-European style, with a garlic and marjoram rub and an apple and celery stuffing. It goes beautifully with braised red cabbage on a cold winter's day. Save the fat that renders from the duck during the cooking process for wonderfully crisp roast potatoes.

Serves 4

1 x 2–2½ kg duck
3 eating apples, peeled and chopped into cubes
1 celery stick, finely chopped
2 tablespoons vegetable oil
freshly ground salt and black pepper
3 garlic cloves, peeled
a handful of fresh marjoram or oregano, finely chopped

Place the duck in the sink and pour over a kettleful of boiling water. Remove and pat the skin dry with kitchen paper and place the duck on a plate. Set aside, uncovered, in the fridge overnight to dry out.

The following day, preheat the oven to 190°C/gas mark 5. To make the stuffing, gently fry the apple pieces and celery in the oil until they just begin to soften. Season with salt and pepper. Set aside to cool.

To prepare the duck, stuff the cooled apple and celery mixture into the cavity. Massage the skin with about 2 teaspoons salt and plenty of black pepper. Pound the garlic with the herbs in a pestle and mortar and mix to a paste with a little olive oil. Smear over the duck skin and prick the duck breast all over with a fork. Place the duck on a rack in a roasting tin and roast for 1½–1¾ hours, or until the juices run clear when you prick the leg and breast with a skewer. You will need to drain the baking tray of excess cooking fat 2–3 times during cooking. Reserve the fat for roast potatoes.

Once the duck is cooked, remove it from the oven and leave to rest for at least 20 minutes before carving. Serve with roast potatoes and braised red cabbage.

6: Vegetables

Historically, Jewish mothers concocted glorious vegetable-rich dishes out of necessity. Families ate vegetables with pulses, potatoes and grains, flavoured with a little goose or chicken fat, as they were cheap and able to withstand slow, overnight cooking. A few chicken bones or scraps of meat were reserved for the Sabbath or Jewish holidays. Here the legacy of these delicious dishes (now flavoured with olive oil and vegetable stock) continues, making them perfect vegetarian main meals. Hopefully you will find new inspiration in this large vegetarian section. For now we understand that we should be lowering our meat intake and following our ancestors by enjoying more grains and pulses, together with masses of seasonal, fresh vegetables that are local if possible. This will in turn reward us with better health, a new vitality, lower costs and the satisfaction of knowing that we are helping preserve the planet's resources.

Roasted Butternut Squash Risotto ⓜ

Butternut squash – revered like the pumpkin for its glorious golden colour – represents the colour of money, and is in season at the time of the Jewish New Year and harvest festival. The Italian Jewish community created butternut squash risotto as part of their repertoire and it melds perfectly with early autumn sage leaves. Often the squash is chopped and added with the rice at the start, or poached in stock and puréed to add at the end, but here I have roasted it with onion and garlic first to intensify the flavour.

Serves 4

450g butternut squash, chopped into 1.5cm cubes
1 large onion, finely chopped
2 garlic cloves, crushed but left whole (green centre removed)
2 tablespoons olive oil
freshly ground salt and black pepper
1.4 litres vegetable stock
120ml white wine
400g risotto rice, such as Arborio or Carnaroli
15g fresh sage, finely chopped
50g grated Parmesan

Preheat the oven to 180°C/gas mark 4. Place the butternut squash, onion and garlic in a roasting tin. Add 1 tablespoon oil and shake to coat. Season well with salt and pepper and roast in the oven for about 40 minutes, or until the squash is golden and starting to brown around the edges. Remove the garlic, squeeze out the succulent flesh and set aside on a little saucer.

Place the vegetable stock in a largish pan and bring to a simmer. Add the wine. Place the remaining tablespoon olive oil in a large, heavy-based pan. Set over a medium heat, add the rice and sage and stir gently to coat the grains in the oil and sage. Once the rice starts to sizzle, add a large ladleful of the hot stock. Keep stirring until all the liquid is absorbed. Add the rest of the hot stock in the same way, one ladleful at a time, waiting for the liquid to be absorbed before adding any more. The rice is cooked when all the stock has been absorbed and the rice is translucent – about 20–25 minutes. Stir in the roasted squash mixture, the reserved roasted garlic and the Parmesan, and serve immediately.

Variations
Add a finely chopped chilli to the roasting tin with the squash. Substitute the rice with pearl barley that you have pre-cooked for one hour in stock.

Leek and Pea Pie

This delicious quiche-style 'pie' (which is made without pastry) has evolved in the Middle East as a wonderful meatless meal.

Serves 6–8 as a main course

400g leeks, sliced and washed really well
2 large onions, peeled and sliced
1 tablespoon olive oil
25g fresh chives, finely chopped
25g fresh flat-leaf parsley or coriander, finely chopped
1 vegetable stock cube
6 organic free-range eggs, plus 6 organic free-range egg yolks
225ml milk
500g frozen peas
freshly ground salt and black pepper
150g grated cheese of your choice

Preheat the oven to 180°C/gas mark 4. In a large frying pan, gently sweat the leeks and onions in the olive oil until soft but not coloured. When they are tender and sweet, add the herbs and crumble in the stock cube. (If you wish, you can process the mixture at this stage for a smooth texture.) Beat the eggs, egg yolks, milk and peas together in a mixing bowl or jug. Pour over the vegetable mixture and season to taste. Tip into a deep 2-litre decorative flan dish and sprinkle with the cheese. Bake in the oven for about 40 minutes until golden and set.

Variation
Add 400g cooked mushrooms to the mixture, or substitute the peas for 250g blanched asparagus, cut into 5cm pieces. For a non-dairy alternative, substitute full-fat coconut milk for the cows' milk and omit the cheese topping.

Spicy Aubergine and Coconut Curry

I've always adored curries and dreamt of visiting Cochin to meet one of the Jewish Indian communities. Paying homage, here is my curry recipe – a fragrant, gentle curry that is not too spicy. Vary the vegetables according to the seasons.

Serves 4–6

2 medium aubergines
2 tablespoons sunflower oil
1 large onion, roughly chopped
1 teaspoon ground coriander
1 teaspoon ground turmeric
1 teaspoon garam masala
1 green chilli (left whole for a milder taste or finely chopped for extra heat)
1 garlic clove, peeled and crushed with 1 teaspoon salt
1 medium cauliflower, cut into florets
a pinch of saffron strands, steeped in 100ml hot water
1 x 400ml tin light coconut milk
12 curry leaves
50g fresh coriander, finely chopped

Preheat the oven to 180°C/gas mark 4. Cut the aubergine into rough chunks, place in a roasting tin and drizzle over 1 tablespoon sunflower oil. Bake in the oven for 40 minutes until nicely charred and tender. (You can always do this in advance.) Set aside.

Heat the remaining tablespoon oil in a large pan with a tight-fitting lid. Add the onion and fry gently over a low heat until soft but not coloured. Stir in the ground coriander, turmeric, garam masala and chilli and cook for a minute or so to release their aroma. Now add the crushed garlic, aubergine, cauliflower and saffron water. Bring to the boil, stirring gently, put on a lid and turn down the heat to low. Simmer gently for about 10 minutes, then add the coconut milk, curry leaves and half of the chopped coriander. Give everything a quick stir and leave to simmer for a further 15 minutes, with the lid off until fragrant and creamy. Garnish with fresh coriander and accompany with basmati rice.

Spicy Vegetable and Potato Tagine

Sitting in a tiny blue synagogue in Morocco was a humbling experience. I felt our shared connections through piles of prayer books, embroidered tallit bags and the everlasting light. Later on, in a Marrakech kitchen, I was shown how to make a good tagine and now I share it with you – spicy and redolent with happy memories.

Serves 4

8 shallots, finely chopped
3 large leeks, trimmed, cut into 8cm lengths and washed really well
1 tablespoon olive oil
8 small carrots (about 500g), peeled and cut into 8cm lengths
500g fresh tomatoes
1 x 450g tin tomatoes
500g waxy potatoes (such as Desiree), peeled and cut into 3cm chunks
2 teaspoons paprika
1 teaspoon ground ginger
½ teaspoon ground black pepper
¼–½ teaspoon cayenne pepper
a large pinch of saffron strands, steeped in 100ml hot water
½ teaspoon ground turmeric
1 vegetable stock cube
4 medium courgettes (about 400g), peeled and cut into 8cm lengths
25g fresh flat-leaf parsley, finely chopped
25g fresh coriander, finely chopped
1 teaspoon sugar (optional)
salt, to taste
10 green olives

In a large pot (I use a pressure cooker like my Moroccan teacher), fry the shallots and leeks over a low in the oil until soft. Add the carrots, fresh tomatoes, tinned tomatoes and potatoes and stir well to coat them in the oil. Add the spices and 400ml water and crumble in the stock cube. Bring to the boil, put on a lid and simmer gently over a lowish heat for 10 minutes. Throw in the courgettes and half of the chopped herbs and give everything a good stir. Season to taste with salt (and a teaspoon of sugar, if the tomatoes are tart) and simmer for a further 5 minutes, with the lid off, until the mixture is meltingly soft and spicy. (If necessary, cook for a further 5 minutes to thicken the sauce.)

To serve, scatter over the olives and garnish with the remaining chopped herbs. Accompany with rice or couscous.

Savoury Vegetable and Noodle Kugel

A healthier version of an old favourite – pasta bake. Now my grandchildren eat spinach!

Serves 8

700g dried pasta shapes (such as penne or rigatoni)
400g fresh spinach
100ml vegetable stock
2 medium onions, roughly chopped
2 teaspoons olive oil
25g fresh flat-leaf parsley
300g low-fat soft cheese
3 organic free-range eggs
200g frozen peas
1 red chilli, finely chopped (optional)
freshly ground salt and black pepper
300g hard cheese of your choice, for the topping

Preheat the oven to 180°C/gas mark 4. Cook the pasta according to the instructions on the packet. Drain into colander and tip back into the pan, keeping a couple of tablespoons of the cooking liquid. Meanwhile, place the spinach in a large pan with the vegetable stock and cook until it wilts. Drain, squeezing out as much liquid as possible, and set aside.

In a large frying pan, gently fry the onion in the oil until soft but not coloured. Tip into a food-processor, add the cooked spinach and parsley and blitz to a smooth green purée. Add the cream cheese and eggs and process quickly to blend. Scoop the spinach mixture into the pan with the pasta, add the peas and chilli (if using) and mix thoroughly to combine. Season well with plenty of salt and black pepper. Tip into an oven-to-table dish, grate over the cheese and bake in the oven for about 45 minutes until golden. Serve with a tomato salad.

Stuffed Onions

When onions are hollowed out, they can be stuffed with all manner of ingredients – vegetarian and meat – to form a substantial starter or light lunch. This recipe uses mushrooms, chopped chestnuts and red wine, but you could use tomatoes and rice with lentils, a spicy curry, a mixture of sausages and red beans – or even some leftover minced meat with a herby seasoning. The results will be glorious.

Serves 6 as a substantial starter or light lunch

6 large onions
about 600ml vegetable stock
25g dried porcini or wild mushrooms
100ml red wine
450g fresh wild mushrooms (or button mushrooms)
1 tablespoon olive oil, plus extra for drizzling
freshly ground salt and black pepper
a pinch of fresh thyme leaves
25g fresh flat-leaf parsley, finely chopped
1 tablespoon cornflour
1 x 245g tin peeled chestnuts, roughly chopped
2 garlic cloves, peeled and crushed (optional)
75g grated cheese of your choice or breadcrumbs (optional)

Preheat the oven to 180°C/gas mark 4. Peel the onions and cut off the bases so they don't topple over. Arrange them in the bottom of a large saucepan and pour over enough vegetable stock to cover. Bring to the boil and simmer gently for about 15 minutes until they are tender enough for you to insert a knife easily. Meanwhile, place the porcini mushrooms in a bowl, pour over the red wine and set aside to soak. Carefully remove the onions from the pan and arrange them in a deepish oven-to-table dish. (Reserve the cooking liquid for soup or stock.)

Chop the fresh mushrooms quite finely and gently fry them in the olive oil until tender. Meanwhile, carefully remove most of the centres from the onions (leaving the outside intact) and blitz to a smooth purée in a food-processor. Season the fried mushrooms with salt and pepper, stir in the herbs and set aside. Strain the porcini mushrooms, reserving the red wine. Combine the wine with the cornflour in a largish saucepan and mix until smooth. Set over a low heat, add the finely chopped porcini mushrooms and stir gently until the mixture thickens. Add the puréed onions, fried mushrooms, chopped chestnuts and garlic (if using) and season to taste. Pack the mixture into the onion cavities and brush with a little olive oil. Grate over the cheese or sprinkle with breadcrumbs (if using). Bake in the oven for 30–40 minutes until tender. Serve with a spinach salad and some crusty granary bread.

CABBAGE

Cabbages, which are cheap and easy to grow, have always been an integral part of both Ashkenazi and Sephardic cuisines.

Cabbage Holishkes

Here individual cabbage leaves are stuffed with a meat and rice or vegetable filling. Holishkes are traditionally made for the Jewish New Year when some Rabbonim believe we should show extra respect, so the cabbage symbolises a veil of reverence concealing the stuffing. Similarly the meat filling in kreplach (see page 62), which is traditionally made for the meal before or after the Day of Atonement, is masked by a layer of dough.
Serves 6–8

1 large or 2 medium cabbages
½ quantity of Tomato Sauce (see page 134)

For the vegetable stuffing
200g lentils of your choice
50g pine nuts
3 medium to large onions (about 450g), roughly chopped
1 tablespoon olive oil
200g risotto rice, such as Arborio or Carnaroli or short-grain brown rice
2 teaspoons vegetable bouillon powder
1 tablespoon tomato purée
50g currants
freshly ground salt and black pepper
½ teaspoon ground allspice
½ teaspoon ground cinnamon
25g fresh mint, finely chopped
25g fresh dill, finely chopped

Preheat the oven to 180°C/gas mark 4. Cook the lentils according to the instructions on the packet. Meanwhile, make the tomato sauce. Toast the pine nuts for the filling in a dry frying pan over a low heat.

In a large, heavy-based pan, gently fry the onion in the olive oil until soft – about 10 minutes. Add the risotto rice and stir to coat the grains in the oil. Add the rest of the ingredients and stir in 250ml water. Set over a low heat and simmer gently for 20 minutes until the rice is cooked and the liquid has been absorbed. Add the lentils and pine nuts, taste and re-season if necessary.

Meanwhile, bring a pan of boiling salted water to the boil. Separate the cabbage leaves and blanch them in the boiling water for 2–3 minutes until just cooked. Drain on kitchen paper.

To assemble the holishkes, open out the cabbage leaves and cut out any thick fibrous ribs. Place 1 tablespoon of the rice filling inside each leaf and roll up tightly, tucking in the ends. You might want to wear rubber gloves because the filling will be hot. Place the filled leaves in an ovenproof dish and cover with the tomato sauce. Bake in the oven for about 20–30 minutes until the leaves are tender. Serve with a cucumber salad.

Variation
Instead of cooking the filled holishkes in tomato sauce, cover them with vegetable stock and interleave them with slices of fresh lemon. For a meat filling, combine leftover pieces of boiled or roast chicken with the rice mixture or use the quick variation for meatballs (see page 87).

Persian Spiced Lentil Patties (P)

It started with a fragrant, pink 'Ispahan' rose that tumbled over the kitchen fence. I dried the petals, savouring the scent. Then I discovered advieh, a Persian spice mix some of our ancestors used to spice rice. A basic recipe uses one teaspoon each of ground cinnamon, ground nutmeg and ground rose petals, with half a teaspoon ground cumin. Now my Persian rose petals have evolved into a spice ingredient!

Makes 8–10

300g red lentils
3 shallots, finely chopped
1 tablespoon olive oil
1 red chilli, finely chopped
25g fresh coriander, finely chopped
1 teaspoon advieh seasoning (available from specialist Middle-Eastern shops)
   or ras-el-hanout
2 organic free-range eggs
freshly ground salt and black pepper
140g medium matzo meal
olive oil, for shallow-frying

Place the lentils in a glass bowl, cover with double the volume of water and cook in the microwave on high for 30 minutes. (Alternatively, simmer them gently in a pan on the hob until tender, topping up with water as necessary to stop them drying out.) Drain any excess liquid. Set aside to cool.

Meanwhile, gently fry the shallots in the olive oil until soft but not coloured. Add the chilli, coriander and advieh and stir for a few minutes to coat the shallots in the herbs and spices. Break the eggs into a large bowl and beat well with a fork. Add the fried shallots and the cooked lentils and mix thoroughly together. Season with salt and pepper. Stir in the matzo meal to bind and set aside to swell for about 10 minutes.

With wet hands, form the lentil mixture into golfball-sized balls and flatten slightly. Fry the patties in the olive oil for 4–5 minutes on each side until golden. Serve with homemade flatbread (or pitta) and salad.

If necessary, these patties can be cooked in advance and reheated, either in the microwave on high for 2 minutes, or on a baking sheet in a low oven for 5 minutes.

Vegetable Mixed Grill with Mint and Coriander Dressing Ⓟ

Take advantage of the most seasonal vegetables by grilling them on a hotplate or ridged griddle pan. Prepare everything in advance and enjoy the glorious roasted flavour, enhanced by a mint and coriander dressing. Serve with crusty bread to soak up the juices.

Za'atar is a Middle Eastern herb/spice mix, made from sumach, sesame seeds, thyme, parsley, oregano and sea salt. If you can't get hold of any, try combining toasted sesame seeds with thyme, parsley and oregano to create a similar flavour.

Serves 8 as a starter

1 medium aubergine
coarse sea salt, for sprinkling
3 courgettes
2 large red peppers
2 onions
a bunch of asparagus
4 small leeks
3 tablespoons olive oil
1 x 400g tin chickpeas in salted water
25g fresh mint, finely chopped, plus extra to garnish
25g fresh coriander, finely chopped
a pinch of cayenne pepper (optional)
freshly ground black pepper
1 tablespoon za'atar
a handful of olives in brine, roughly chopped
2 tablespoons of capers in brine, roughly chopped

Cut the aubergine into long 1cm-thick slices. Place in a colander in the sink and sprinkle with coarse sea salt. Set aside for 20 minutes to draw out the bitter juices.

Cut the courgettes into slices the same thickness as the aubergine. De-seed the peppers and cut into slices lengthways. Peel the onions and cut into 1cm rings. Carefully wash the asparagus and snap off the woody ends. Split the leeks in half lengthways, open out and wash really well under a running tap. Cut into similar-sized strips. Rinse the aubergines to remove all the salt.

Heat a ridged griddle pan until it is smoking hot. Brush the vegetables with olive oil and place on the hot grill – you may need to do this in batches. Grill for about a minute on each side until they are nicely charred and then transfer to a platter or serving dish. Sprinkle with the chopped olives and capers. Meanwhile, make the dressing by processing the tin of chickpeas (including the liquid) with the mint, coriander, cayenne (if using) and some pepper.

To serve, tip any of the juices from the griddle pan into the dressing, mix thoroughly and drizzle over the vegetables. Sprinkle with fresh mint and za'atar, scatter over some fresh olives and enjoy hot or cold.

Variation
Substitute the za'atar with grated lemon zest.

Stuffed Autumn Vegetables ⓟ

My husband's favourite Sephardic-style recipe incorporates a whole butternut squash, grown with love in his mini-garden to be used for Succoth or harvest festival.

Our biblical ancestors understood the importance of a good harvest. A good crop was cause for a huge Thanksgiving celebration. Interestingly, at that time, farmers lived out in the fields, building themselves temporary booths so they could continue picking. Then later, when they were forced out into the wilderness during the festival of Succoth, they used their knowledge to rebuild those booths. Succoth also signifies the autumn, the final harvest – a chance to relax and enjoy the season's produce.

Serves 4–6

50g pine nuts
1 large butternut squash or marrow (about 1kg)
1 tablespoon olive oil, plus extra for brushing
freshly ground salt and black pepper
250g green lentils
250g brown rice
2 large onions, roughly chopped
2 garlic cloves, peeled and crushed
50g currants
15g fresh dill, finely chopped
25g fresh coriander, finely chopped
1 tablespoon paprika
1 teaspoon ground cinnamon
2 tablespoons tomato purée
about 2 tablespoons Kiddush wine

Preheat the oven to 170°C/gas mark 3. Scatter the pine nuts on a baking sheet and toast in the oven for 5 minutes until golden. Keep an eye on them because they can burn easily. Set aside.

Increase the oven temperature to 180°C/gas mark 4. Cut the squash or marrow in half, scoop out the seeds and discard. Make criss-cross cuts into the flesh and brush the edges with a little oil. Season well with salt and pepper and place in a roasting tin. Bake in the oven for 30 minutes.

Meanwhile, place the lentils in a saucepan, cover with double the volume of water and simmer for 30 minutes until tender, topping up as necessary with more water. Place the rice in a separate pan, cover again with twice the volume of water and simmer for 40 minutes. Drain and set aside.

In a large saucepan, gently fry the onion in the oil until soft but not coloured. Stir in the garlic, then add the lentils, rice and the remaining ingredients. Season with salt and pepper and taste, adding more seasoning or Kiddush wine if necessary.

Remove the squash from the oven, fill the cavities with the lentil and rice mixture and return to the oven for a further 30 minutes, or until the squash is very soft.

Variations

For a meaty version, add some chopped cooked meat or leftover chicken to the rice and lentil mixture. For a stronger flavour, boil 1 large onion for 30 minutes to tenderise it, and then chop the flesh and add to the mixture. Accompany with a rich tomato sauce (see page 134).

Carrot and Honey Tzimmes (P)

Tzimmes (which means 'a confused or muddled state' in Yiddish) is a star of Jewish cuisine and its flavour has even coloured our literature. Faye Moskowitz, in her book *And the Bridge is Love*, describes Aunt Celia with 'red hair the colour of carrot tzimmes cooked in honey and darkened with cinnamon.'

Serves 4–5

500g carrots, peeled and cut into 1½ cm rings
1 cooking apple, peeled and cut into slices
1 medium sweet potato, peeled and cut into slices
1 large eating apple, peeled and cut into slices
1 tablespoon honey
1 teaspoon mixed spice
1 teaspoon ground cinnamon
grated zest and juice of 1 orange or 2 clementines
50ml apple juice or water

Preheat the oven to 180°C/gas mark 4. Combine the ingredients in an oven-to-table dish and bake in the oven for at least an hour until all the vegetables are tender. Serve alongside meat or even as a dessert.

Variation

For a meaty version, lay a piece of beef brisket in the bottom of your dish and cover with a layer of sliced onions. Spread the carrot mixture on top and pour over enough hot stock or water to cover. Cover with foil and bake in the oven at 150°C/gas mark 2 for 6–8 hours (preferably overnight), topping up with water as necessary.

For dried fruit tzimmes, combine 150g each chopped prunes, apricots and dates, 150g raisins and 150g pearl barley in a large, heavy-based saucepan. Squeeze over the juice of 1 orange and 1 lemon and grate over the zest. Top up with 2 litres hot stock or water and simmer gently over a low heat for at least an hour (but preferably overnight) until sweetly tender.

Hot Spiced Cabbage

This delicious dish, with onion and caraway flavours, enhances the simple cabbage, turning it into a delicacy that can be served with meat, fish or parve recipes.

Serves 4–6 as a side dish

1 medium cabbage, shredded
1 onion, finely chopped
1 tablespoon olive oil
1 tablespoon caraway seeds
200ml vegetable or chicken stock (depending on the meal served)
freshly ground salt and black pepper

Carefully wash the cabbage and check for insects. In a large pan, gently fry the onion in the oil until soft but not coloured. Add the cabbage, caraway seeds and stock and stir well to combine. Place the lid on the pan and cook over a low heat for 10–15 minutes, shaking the pan from time to time. Season with salt and pepper and serve as a tasty vegetable alongside meat or fish.

Sweet and Sour Red Cabbage

My late father adored this recipe, fondly prepared for him by my mother.

Serves 4–6 as a side dish

1 medium red cabbage, shredded
1 onion, finely chopped
1 tablespoon olive oil
2 garlic cloves, peeled and crushed
1 large pear or Braeburn apple, peeled and chopped into pieces
1 cinnamon stick
1–2 tablespoons apple cider vinegar
1 tablespoon soft dark brown sugar
25g raisins
a couple of sprigs of fresh thyme
10g caraway seeds (optional)
freshly ground salt and black pepper

Carefully wash the cabbage and check for insects. In a large pan, gently fry the onions in the oil until soft but not coloured. Add the garlic and stir to release its flavour. Put in the shredded cabbage, along with all the other ingredients expect for the salt and pepper. Give the mixture a really good stir and put on a lid. Cook over a low heat for 20–25 minutes until the cabbage is soft and thick in texture, stirring from time to time. Season to taste.

Mushrooms and Chestnuts in Red Wine Sauce with Fluffy Mustard Mash

I created this recipe for a television programme and was delighted when it satisfied confirmed carnivores.
Serves 4

For the stew ⓟ
2 large onions, peeled and chopped
2 tablespoons olive oil
240g wild or chestnut mushrooms
1 x 240g tin organic chestnuts, roughly chopped
a few sprigs of fresh thyme
120ml red wine
1 heaped tablespoon cornflour
2 teaspoons vegetable bouillon powder
freshly ground salt and black pepper

For the mash Ⓜ
4 large potatoes, scrubbed but left whole
a knob of butter
75ml milk
2 teaspoons wholegrain mustard

Place the (unpeeled) potatoes in a large pan, cover with water and cook until tender.

In a large frying pan, gently fry the onions in the oil until soft and just starting to colour. Add the mushrooms and fry until tender. Throw in the chestnuts and thyme and add the wine. In a small bowl, combine the cornflour with the vegetable stock powder and mix to a paste with 3–4 tablespoons cold water. Add the cornflour mixture to the pan and stir well to combine. Bring to the boil and simmer for 10 minutes.

Meanwhile, drain the potatoes and peel off the skins – they will be hot, so wear rubber gloves. Mash the flesh or push it through a potato ricer back into the pan. Add the butter, milk and mustard, season with salt and pepper and beat with a wooden spoon until fluffy.

To serve, season the mushroom mixture with salt and pepper and serve with a spoonful of mustard mash on the side.

Potato Kugel

Potato kugel has been a mainstay of traditional Ashkenazi cookery. In the past, kugels often had a leaden, gluey, greyish inside. My mission was to change that image and bring the now golden potato kugel crisply and joyfully into the 21st century.

Serves 8

2 small or 1 medium onion, roughly chopped
2 tablespoons olive oil
500g waxy potatoes (such as Jersey Royals or Charlotte),
    scrubbed and left whole
25g fresh flat-leaf parsley
4 organic free-range eggs
1½ tablespoons lemon juice
2kg floury potatoes (such as Desiree)
4 tablespoons ground almonds
2 teaspoons sugar
1 teaspoon salt
plenty of freshly ground black pepper

Preheat the oven to 170°C/gas mark 3 and grease a large rectangular tin, 26 x 34cm. Alternatively you can line with baking parchment.

In a small frying pan, gently fry the onion in 1 tablespoon of the oil until soft but not coloured. Meanwhile, parboil the waxy potatoes in their skins for about 15 minutes until almost tender but not soft. Drain and set aside. Tip the softened onion into a food-processor, add the parsley and eggs and blitz until smooth. Scrape into a large bowl and stir in the lemon juice. (If you don't have a processor, simply finely chop the parsley and mix with the beaten eggs and cooked onion.)

Peel the floury potatoes and grate them on the coarse side of a grater into the bowl with the lemon and egg mixture. Mix well with your hands, taking care that the potato is coated with the lemon and egg mixture; the lemon will stop the potato oxidising and going black. Mix in the ground almonds, sugar and salt and pour into the prepared tin. Thickly slice the waxy potatoes and arrange them over the top. Brush with the remaining oil and season with more salt and pepper. Bake in the oven for about 1 hour until slightly puffed up and golden.

Variations

Mashed Potato Kugel

For mashed potato kugel, omit the waxy potatoes and use 2.5kg floury potatoes instead. Peel the potatoes and boil them in water or stock until tender. Drain, season and mash until smooth. Meanwhile, slice 2 large onions and gently fry them in 1 tablespoon olive oil until soft but not coloured. Set aside to cool and then beat in 4 egg yolks. Combine the onion and egg mixture with the mashed potato. Whisk 4 egg whites until stiff and fold in carefully. Spoon the mixture into a greased dish, top with grated cheese (optional – only for a *milchig* meal) and bake in a low oven for 1 hour as before.

Potato Pompoms

These crisp, golden baked balls are the easiest recipe in the world! Season leftover mashed potato with plenty of salt and pepper, but do not add milk or butter. Form into large balls, about the size of a tennis ball. Arrange on a baking tray, drizzle with olive oil and bake at 180°C/gas mark 4 for 1 hour. (If you have a surplus of mashed potato, simply open-freeze the formed pompoms ready to bake another day.)

Latkes

This recipe is exceptional because it uses matzo meal and baking powder to soak up the juice from the grated potato. This adds flavour and fluffiness to the dish, while still retaining all of the nutritional value of the potato.

Makes 56 smallish latkes

1 red onion, cut into quarters
5 organic free-range eggs
1.25kg large floury potatoes (such as Desiree), skins on, scrubbed and cut into
    rough chunks
110g medium matzo meal
a pinch of baking powder
freshly ground salt and black pepper
vegetable oil, for shallow-frying

Place the onion in a food-processor and blitz until smooth. Add the eggs and blitz again. Pour into a large mixing bowl. Grate the potato coarsely – you can either do this with a vegetable grater, or by changing the blade in your food-processor. Tip the grated potato, along with any liquid, into the bowl with the onions and eggs. Stir in the matzo meal and baking powder and season with salt and pepper.

To cook the latkes, pour vegetable oil into two separate frying pans until they are half full. Using two pans will make the process much quicker. Heat the oil until it is hot but not smoking and then drop tablespoonfuls of the mixture carefully into the pans, to make small, round patties. Cook for about 5 minutes on each side until golden and crisp, and then drain on kitchen paper while you cook the rest.

Variations

For a spicy, oriental twist, add 1 chilli, deseeded and chopped, a thumb-sized piece of grated fresh root ginger and a large handful of finely chopped fresh coriander.

For a sweeter flavour, omit the onion, use sweet potatoes in place of regular potatoes and season with cinnamon or mixed spice. Dust with icing sugar and serve with a spoonful of apple sauce and a generous dollop of soured cream. This unusual combination is often seen in Ashkenazi cooking where sweet is served with savoury – and harks back to medieval times.

Spiced Onion and Vegetable Pakoras ⓟ

In Jewish eyes, this could be termed as a latke with attitude! I include these glorious spiced fritters as homage to the Jews of Cochin. They came as traders from Judea in 562BCE, and others followed after the destruction of the temple in 70CE. Later more Jews arrived, this time persecuted by the Portuguese for their involvement in the pepper trade. Today the very small community enjoys vegetarian, fish and chicken-based recipes, since they no longer have a shochet to kill beasts.

You can prepare these spicy pakoras in advance and reheat them. Control the spice level by reducing the chilli content. It's an unusual recipe to serve to vegetarians or, indeed, as a latke substitute, and as it contains so many vegetables, it is the perfect way to persuade children to enjoy their five-a-day.

Makes 6–8

1 large potato, scrubbed
140g gram flour
½ teaspoon baking powder
1 teaspoon salt
a pinch of ground turmeric
½ teaspoon ground chilli powder
1 green chilli, finely chopped (optional)
1 large onion, finely sliced
1 large carrot, peeled
25g fresh coriander, finely chopped
2.5cm piece of fresh root ginger, peeled and finely grated
1 garlic clove, peeled and crushed (optional)
vegetable oil, for deep-frying

Cook the potato in boiling water until just cooked, and then set aside to cool. Sift the flour into a large bowl and combine with the baking powder, salt, turmeric and chilli powder. Pour in 115ml water, whisking all the time to give a smooth, thickish batter. Add the chopped chilli (if using). Set aside to stand for about 20 minutes.

Meanwhile, grate the potato and carrot on the coarse side of a grater into a bowl. Add the onion, coriander, ginger and garlic, and mix well. Add to the batter and combine thoroughly.

To cook the pakoras, heat the oil in a wide, deepish pan. Wait for the oil to reach 190°C and then carefully drop in heaped tablespoons of the vegetable mixture – you will need to do this in batches. Cook on each side until golden and crisp, and then drain on kitchen paper while you cook the rest.

Serve hot with a cooling sauce made from 150g plain yoghurt mixed with 125g peeled and finely chopped cucumber, and 15g finely chopped fresh mint.

Shakshuka

Shakshuka has become part of the Israeli way of life. Eggs have always been comparatively cheap in Israel and combining them with easily-grown tomatoes, garlic and oil makes for the ideal brunch recipe. This recipe is similar to the Moroccan version, although the Moroccans would traditionally cook it in a simple tagine.

Serves 8

1kg fresh tomatoes, roughly chopped
4 garlic cloves, peeled and crushed
1 tablespoon tomato purée
1 tablespoon olive oil
salt and freshly ground black pepper
2 teaspoons sweet paprika
1 teaspoon salt
8 organic free-range eggs

Place the tomatoes, garlic, tomato purée, oil, salt, pepper and paprika in a deep-sided frying pan over a medium heat. Simmer for 10 minutes and continue stirring until the tomatoes soften and you have a tasty sauce. Carefully break the eggs, one at a time, into a glass to check for blood spots, and then carefully lower them into the sauce. Depending on your preference, you can either break the yolk (which is traditional) or leave it whole. Simmer for a further 5 minutes to cook the eggs, and then take the pan to the table for everyone to help themselves.

Variations
Add some chopped fresh herbs – basil or coriander – at the end, or a handful of stoned olives (not traditional but delicious). To make the dish more substantial (and *milchig*), scatter over a handful of cubed feta cheese or serve with cottage cheese.

Homemade Tomato Sauce

This delicious and versatile sauce recipe is wonderful served over pasta, gnocchi or as a pizza topping. It freezes perfectly, so it is always worth making extra to have on standby.

Serves 16 as a pasta sauce

1 tablespoon olive oil
2 large or 4 small onions (about 450g), roughly chopped
2 garlic cloves, crushed (optional)
1kg fresh tomatoes
3 celery sticks, finely chopped
2 x 400g tins chopped tomatoes
25g fresh oregano, roughly chopped
50g fresh flat-leaf parsley, roughly chopped
2 teaspoons ground paprika
1 teaspoon sugar
50g fresh basil

Sweat the onions in the olive oil until soft but not coloured. Add the garlic (if using), along with the rest of the ingredients except the basil, and simmer gently until the celery is tender – about 15 minutes. Tip the mixture into a food-processor, add the basil and blend until smooth. This version retains all the seeds and skins, providing masses of fibre. However, if you prefer a smoother sauce you can pass it through a sieve after blending. This freezes very well in small containers.

Mujadara

This glorious dish of spiced rice and lentils, enhanced by fried onions, is served up in Sephardi communities from Syria and Egypt. The combination of grain and pulse is now acclaimed by nutritionists as a perfect balance. Try to obtain good cinnamon for this – I grind pieces of cinnamon bark for a super fragrant taste.

Serves 6–8

225g green lentils
225g brown rice
3 large onions (about 500g), peeled and sliced
1 tablespoon olive oil
1 tablespoon ground cinnamon
1 tablespoon ground cumin
freshly ground salt and black pepper
a handful of fresh mint or coriander, to garnish (optional)

Tahini sauce
4 heaped tablespoons Greek yogurt
2 tablespoons tahini paste
grated zest and juice of ½ lemon
¼ teaspoon ground cumin
2 tablespoons za'atar
salt

Place the green lentils in a pan, cover with double the volume of water and simmer for about 40–50 minutes until soft and tender, topping up with water as necessary to stop them drying out. Place the rice in a separate pan, cover with twice the volume of water and simmer for 40 minutes until tender. Drain and set aside.

Gently fry the onions in the oil on a very low heat – the aim is to caramelise them as slowly as possible. This will take about 20 minutes. Add the spices and stir for 2–3 minutes to release their aroma. Add the drained lentils and rice and mix well to combine. Season with salt and pepper.

To make the tahini sauce, combine all the ingredients in a little bowl. To serve, spoon the mujadara into serving bowls, garnish with the finely chopped mint or coriander (if using) and accompany with the tahini sauce.

Barley Tabbouleh

This gentle twist on a Middle-Eastern salad uses barley – a valuable, low-GI wholegrain. Tabbouleh makes a satisfying summer salad that will sit happily next to a piece of grilled fish or wurst, and can be served up the next day in a lunchbox.

Serves 4 as a side dish

200g pearl or pot barley
675ml vegetable stock
1 tablespoon olive oil
grated zest of 1 lemon, plus 2 tablespoons lemon juice
freshly ground salt and black pepper
1 garlic clove, peeled and crushed
3 spring onions, finely chopped
25g fresh mint, finely chopped
25g fresh flat-leaf parsley, finely chopped
3 large tomatoes, finely chopped
60g chopped pistachios or toasted pine nuts (optional)

Place the barley in a saucepan, cover with the stock and simmer gently for 1 hour for pearl barley, or 1½–2 hours for pot barley.

While hot, add the oil, lemon zest and juice and some salt and pepper and set aside to cool. When the mixture is cool, add the rest of the ingredients and combine well. Enjoy!

Variation

Substitute the barley for quinoa and cook according to the instructions on the packet – this is easy in the microwave. Quinoa is a delicious, high-protein food that is not a grain and therefore suitable for people who are allergic to grains.

Moroccan Cooked Carrot Salad ⓟ

This delicious salad, taught to me by Malika in Fez, turns a simple carrot into a heavenly feast. Perfect served with any meal, this is a great way of adding spice simply and cheaply.
Serves 4–6

500g fresh carrots, peeled and
   chopped into 1cm rings or sticks
1 teaspoon ground cumin
1 teaspoon paprika
⅛ teaspoon cayenne pepper
grated zest and juice of ½ lemon
1 teaspoon olive oil
25g fresh coriander, finely chopped
25g fresh parsley or mint, finely chopped
freshly ground salt and black pepper

Cook the carrots gently with the spices in a minimum of water until tender. Add the lemon zest and juice, olive oil and fresh herbs. Season to taste and leave to cool.

7: Desserts

For special occasions, there is nothing more evocative of the past than traditional Jewish puddings – the ultimate comfort food. Good times shared are woven into memories of lokshen pudding (sweet vanilla-rich noodles, studded with vine fruits); a spiced, flaky apfel strudel; chocolate mousse with a hint of brandy, and the perfect apple pie topped with a crisp, sparkling crust of sugar crystals.

APPLES

'Comfort me with apples', says the Song of Songs. Some say the apple was the fruit of the Tree of Knowledge and certainly its sweet/sharpness and rich colour speak of a gorgeous voluptuousness. The lump on the larynx – prominent on the man's throat – is called the Adam's apple, symbolising the piece of apple that stuck in his throat during the Fall. And surely our best childhood recollection has to be dipping apple slices in honey for a sweet, good year.

Sticky Toffee Apple Pudding for Rosh Hashanah Ⓟ or Ⓜ

This sticky toffee honey pudding is enriched with the tartness of cooking apples for the perfect Yom Tov dessert.
Serves 8–10

225g plain flour
¾ teaspoon bicarbonate of soda
½ teaspoon ground cinnamon
120g dairy-free margarine or butter
120g fairtrade dark brown muscovado sugar
150ml honey (or golden syrup)
2 organic free-range eggs
4 tablespoons soya milk or whole milk
1 cooking apple
juice and grated zest of ½ lemon
8 dates, stoned and finely chopped
60g crystallised or stem ginger, finely chopped (optional)

Preheat the oven to 170°C/gas mark 3 and line a 21cm round, loose-bottomed cake tin with parchment paper.

Sift the flour with the bicarbonate of soda and cinnamon into a bowl. Melt the margarine with the muscovado sugar and honey (or golden syrup) in a small pan. Set aside to cool slightly. Beat the eggs with the milk in a large mixing bowl. Peel and grate the apple and mix with the lemon zest and juice. Combine with the egg mixture and stir in the dates and ginger (if using). Pour in the melted honey mixture and combine thoroughly. Quickly fold in the flour and spices and spoon into the prepared tin.

Bake in the oven for about 1 hour until the cake is gloriously golden brown and risen. Insert a skewer – it should come out clean if cooked. Serve hot or cold with ice cream and enjoy for a sweet, good year. This dessert keeps for days and remains sticky and moreish.

PASTRY IN ALL ITS GLORY

'A chef who has no knowledge of pastry is a chef with only one arm.'
JEAN ANTHELME BRILLAT-SAVARIN

There are fascinating Jewish explanations for pastry's popularity, entwined with religious references. The Shulchan Aruch tells of manna from heaven, which explains why bourekas are eaten on Friday night: 'since the filling is covered by pastry above and below, like the manna which was protected by dew above and beneath it.'

In medieval times, Jewish people surrounded by superstition would write a wish on a piece of paper, wrap it in dough and attach it to a piece of string to wear around their necks as a talisman.

The religious sages of old believed Jewish lives were directed by outside forces and that seams of mysticism surrounded and hid that controlling hand. A plain dough, such as a Hamantaschen, is a metaphor for this magical hidden power as it conceals a sweet filling.

Apfel Strudel ⓟ

Creating and pulling real strudel dough is almost considered a lost art. However, recreating a precious recipe gives a huge sense of achievement. The dough is easy to make with the help of a food-processor. Otherwise, use a thin shortcrust or filo pastry to give the magical flake needed.

We have opted for a healthier, but equally delicious, filling of apples with low-sugar marmalade and ground almonds in place of the more traditional melted butter, sugar and breadcrumbs.

Makes 4 strudels

For the strudel dough
420g plain flour, plus extra for dusting
¼ teaspoon salt
3 organic free-range eggs
4 tablespoons light vegetable oil
10g vanilla sugar (optional, for a sweeter dough)

For the spiced apple filling
4–6 eating apples, such as Jonagold
juice and grated zest of 1 lemon
2 teaspoons ground cinnamon or mixed spice
4 tablespoons sugar-free marmalade or black cherry jam
175g ground almonds
175g seedless raisins
1 organic free-range egg, to glaze

First make the strudel dough. Place all the ingredients with 65ml water in a food-processor and mix to smooth, pliable dough. Chill for at least 30 minutes.

Preheat the oven to 190°C/gas mark 5. Divide the dough into four pieces. Roll out the dough as thinly as possible on a floured surface, and then start the pulling process. Stretch the dough into a rectangle by pulling it over your knuckles, turning it as you go. Avoid handling it with your fingertips or you will tear the dough, and try to avoid stretching it in the same area. The dough is ready when it is thin enough to read the newspaper through. Trim away any thick edges with a sharp knife. Roll out the remaining pastry in the same way to give four thin sheets of pastry, about 21 x 20cm. Cover each rolled-out sheet with a clean damp cloth or kitchen roll to prevent it drying out.

To make the strudel filling, grate the apples on the coarse side of a grater into a large bowl – you can peel them if you wish, but I leave the skins on for extra colour and fibre. Add the lemon zest and juice and stir in the cinnamon or mixed spice. Spread each sheet of strudel pastry with a tablespoon of marmalade or jam, leaving a border all around. Divide the grated apple mixture between each one and spread out to cover the marmalade or jam. Sprinkle with the ground almonds and finally a layer of raisins. Glaze the borders with beaten egg and tuck in the two shortest ends. Carefully roll up the strudels to make Swiss-roll shapes and transfer to a lined baking sheet. Glaze with beaten egg. Bake in the oven for 20–30 minutes, or until golden brown. Once cooled, sprinkle with icing sugar to serve.

Variation
As an alternative filling, try grated pear with blueberry jam, or nectarine with raspberry jam.

My Mother Judith's Wonderful Apple Pie Ⓟ or Ⓜ

This cherished recipe uses half self-raising flour and half plain flour to produce a fluffy, cakey pastry. If you prefer a more traditional style, use all plain flour.
Serves 4–6

For the pastry
150g plain flour
150g self-raising flour
150g dairy-free margarine or butter
1 tablespoon peanut butter (optional) – this gives a nutty flavour
100g fairtrade soft light brown sugar
10g vanilla sugar
grated zest of 1 lemon, plus 1–2 teaspoons lemon juice
1 organic free-range egg, beaten

For the filling
700g peeled, cored and sliced apples –
    use half Bramley cooking apples and
    half eating apples such as Jonagold
grated zest and juice of 1 lemon (or orange)
1 teaspoon mixed spice or ground cinnamon
100g sultanas
6 tablespoons chunky marmalade
3 tablespoons ground almonds

For the sparkly topping
5–10g caster sugar

Preheat the oven to 200°C/gas mark 6. Sift the flours into a large mixing bowl and rub in the margarine and peanut butter (if using) with your fingers to form a breadcrumb-like mixture. Stir in the sugars and lemon zest. Add the beaten egg and enough lemon juice to mix to a soft dough. Wrap in clingfilm and chill in the fridge for at least 30 minutes.

To make the filling, combine all the ingredients and spoon into a 1.5-litre pie dish. Roll out the pastry to fit the dish and press down around the edges to seal. Decorate with pastry leaves and sprinkle with caster sugar.

Bake in the oven for 15 minutes, and then turn down the temperature to 180°C/gas mark 4 and cook for a further 30 minutes until gorgeously golden. Serve with custard or parve cream.

Blackcurrant and Almond Tart Ⓟ or Ⓜ

This elegant, almond-based tart is the perfect foil for the sharp fruit, creating a wonderfully sweet/tart dessert.
Serves 10

500g shortcrust pastry or 1 batch of extra-rich shortcrust pastry (see page 145)
180g blackcurrant conserve or jam
2 punnets (about 400g) fresh blackcurrants, de-stalked and washed

For the almond filling
120g ground almonds
120g dairy-free margarine or butter
120g fairtrade soft light brown sugar
2 organic free-range eggs
a drop of almond extract
2 tablespoons vanilla sugar
2 tablespoons cornflour
100g flaked almonds

Preheat the oven to 180°C/gas mark 4. Line a 30cm tart dish with the pastry and spread the base with the blackcurrant conserve. Scatter over the blackcurrants and chill in the fridge while you make the filling.

To make the filling, place all the ingredients, except the flaked almonds, in a food-processor and blitz to a smooth cream. Spoon over the blackcurrants and sprinkle with the flaked almonds. Bake in the oven for 40–50 minutes until golden brown.

Apfel im Schlafrock (apples in dressing gowns) Ⓟ

When I was a child I loved the vision of my mother's apples in their dressing gowns – pastry-covered windfalls enclosing a magical pocket of jam. Because this recipe typically follows a meat meal, the pastry has been reworked so that's it is possible to make it with dairy-free soft margarine. Here a daintier version using nectarines or plums stuffed with marzipan makes an elegant autumn dessert. The juice oozes slightly on cooking but this adds to the charm of the dish.

Makes 8

For the extra-rich shortcrust pastry (or, as my mother called it, 'Mürbeteig')
410g plain flour
a pinch of salt
200g dairy-free soft margarine
130g ground almonds
70g fairtrade soft light brown sugar
30g vanilla sugar
1 organic free-range egg
2 egg yolks – save one egg white for the topping and freeze the other for making meringues or biscuits
1 teaspoon vanilla extract
zest of 1 lemon, grated
1 tablespoon very cold water

For the filling
8 teaspoons jam
4 plums or nectarines, halved
120g marzipan

1 beaten egg white, to glaze
caster sugar, for sprinkling

Sift the flour and salt into a large mixing bowl and rub in the margarine with your fingertips to form fine breadcrumbs. Stir in the ground almonds and sugars. Gradually add the egg and yolks, vanilla extract and lemon zest along with enough water to mix to a delicious soft dough. Wrap in clingfilm and chill in the fridge for at least an hour.

Preheat the oven to 180°C/gas mark 4. On a floured surface, roll out the dough to a thickness of about 1–1.5 mm and cut out 8 x 12cm circles with a fluted cutter. Brush the centre of each circle with a teaspoon of jam. Stone the fruit and place a ball of marzipan In each cavity, then lay the filled fruit face down in the centre of each pastry circle. Score the skin of the fruit 3–4 times, and brush with egg white. Wet the edges of the pastry circle and bring them together in the centre to form a ball around the fruit. For a wonderfully decorative touch, add a pastry leaf cut from any excess pastry. Glaze with the beaten egg white and sprinkle with sugar. Carefully transfer the pastry parcels onto two baking sheets and bake in the oven for 30–35 minutes until golden brown. Serve hot or cold with parve ice cream, cream or custard for a milky treat.

Variation
Substitute good homemade jam or lemon curd for the marzipan.

LOKSHEN PUDDING

Most lokshen puddings are rich and substantial. However, it is possible to recreate a traditional lokshen pudding without sacrificing taste, by cutting down on the fat and sugar. This one is made with soya milk, making it suitable for serving after a meat meal.

Almost Fat-Free Lokshen Pudding (P)

Serves 6

500g lokshen – any noodles will work but angel-hair are traditional
1 teaspoon salt
juice and grated zest of 1 orange
400g dried fruit
2 tablespoons good-quality marmalade or apricot jam
2 tablespoons Kiddush wine (optional)
2 Bramley cooking apples
1 Jonagold eating apple
juice and grated zest of 1 lemon
4 organic free-range eggs
600ml soya milk
1 tablespoon vanilla sugar
2 tablespoons golden caster sugar

Preheat the oven to 180°C/gas mark 4. Cook the noodles in boiling water for 5 minutes, or according to the instructions on the packet. Drain (retaining a little of the cooking water in the pan), season with salt, and leave to cool slightly. In a small pan, heat the orange juice with the dried fruit, marmalade or jam and wine (if using). Simmer for a few minutes to plump up the fruit and then remove from the heat. Grate the apples (including the peel if you wish) into a bowl. Add the lemon juice to stop them discolouring, along with the orange and lemon zest. Beat the eggs with the soya milk and vanilla sugar and tip into the bowl with the apples. Add the soaked dried fruit and noodles and combine thoroughly. Pour into a 2-litre oven-to-table dish. Sprinkle with the golden caster sugar and bake in the oven for about 40 minutes until golden brown.

Rich Lokshen Pudding

Soaking the dried fruit in lemon juice introduces moisture to this traditional pudding, which is flavoured with spices, lemon, orange and vanilla. Using low-fat cream cheese and margarine makes it more healthy, but feel free to use full-fat cheese and butter if you wish.

Serves 4

225g lokshen – any noodles will work but angel-hair are traditional
1 teaspoon salt
300g dried fruit
juice and grated zest of 1 lemon
grated zest of 1 orange
25g low-fat margarine or butter
300g low-fat cream cheese
2 organic free-range eggs, beaten
2 teaspoons vanilla extract
¼ teaspoon mixed spice or ground cinnamon
50g fairtrade soft light or dark brown sugar, to sprinkle

Preheat the oven to 180°C/gas mark 4. Cook the noodles in boiling water for 5 minutes, or according to the instructions on the packet. Drain, season with salt and return to the pan. Place the dried fruit, lemon juice and orange and lemon zest in a small pan and simmer over a low heat for a few minutes to plump up the fruit. Once the fruit is plump and juicy, remove from the heat and set aside to cool slightly. Tip the fruit into the pan with the noodles and stir in the margarine or butter and cheese. Beat in the eggs, vanilla extract and mixed spice or cinnamon. Pour into a 1.5-litre oven-to-table dish and sprinkle with brown sugar. Bake in the oven for 30–40 minutes until golden and crisp.

Variation
Add 2 tablespoons Calvados or brandy to the pan with the dried fruit and lemon juice.

Blueprint for the Perfect Blintz Ⓜ

'And if thy offering be a meal offering baked in a pan, it shall be of fine flour unleavened mingled with oil. Thou shalt break it in pieces and pour oil on thereon.' Leviticus, 2:7

Blintzes are tender, delectable pancakes that are traditionally filled with slightly sweetened, soft cream cheese, sometimes flavoured with lemon zest or dried fruit to cut through the richness. Blintzes originated in Poland and there are as many recipes for them as Jewish mothers! Blinis are their distant cousins, made with a yeast base. Both were traditionally served with extra melted butter. It is said that if the blintzes are served as two rolls of pancake, next to each other, they represent the tablets given to Moses.

Makes 16–18

For the pancake mixture
400g plain flour
a pinch of salt
100g melted butter
800ml whole milk
50ml olive oil
4 organic free-range eggs
a little vegetable or sunflower oil, for frying
icing sugar, for dusting
soured cream, to serve

For the filling
EITHER
350g soft cream cheese
15g vanilla sugar
grated zest of 1 lemon
grated zest of ½ orange
juice of ½ lemon
a pinch of salt

OR
450g cottage cheese
1 organic free-range egg yolk
grated zest of 1 lemon
2 tablespoons lemon juice
seeds of 1 vanilla pod
1 tablespoon honey
½ teaspoon mixed spice or ground cinnamon
100g chopped dried fruit – dates, apricots or raisins

Sift the flour into a large bowl, add the salt and make a well in the centre. Warm the butter in a small pan. Measure the milk into a large measuring jug, add the oil, the melted butter and the eggs and beat well with a fork to combine. Pour the liquid ingredients into the flour, whisking continuously to form a smooth, cream-like batter. (If you end up with lumps, which you shouldn't with this method, simply strain the mixture through a sieve.) Set aside to stand for at least 30 minutes.

Preheat the oven to 180°C/gas mark 4 and grease an oven-to-table dish. To cook the blintzes, heat 1 tablespoon oil in a heavy-based frying pan and swirl it around to cover the base. Tip out any excess oil to reuse again. Using a small ladle, drop a small amount of the batter into the pan and swirl it around, covering the base of the pan, to make a thickish pancake. Wait for small bubbles to appear on the surface and then flip the pancake over to cook on the other side – toss, if you are brave, or flip with a fish-slice if you are not! Cook for 20–30 seconds on the other side and then transfer to a platter lined with kitchen paper. Cook the remaining blintzes in the same way and stack them up in between layers of baking parchment to prevent them from sticking.

To make the filling, beat all the ingredients together until smooth. Place a heaped tablespoon of the filling inside each pancake and roll up. Transfer the filled blitzes to an ovenproof dish and bake in the oven for 15 minutes. To serve, dust with icing sugar and accompany with soured cream on the side.

Extra-Easy Cheat's Crème Brûlée

Practically as good as the real thing, ten times easier and perfect for an almost instant dinner party dessert.
Serves 4

1 punnet (150–170g) blueberries
1 punnet (150–170g) raspberries
1 x 450g tub good-quality vanilla custard
1 x 450g tub set Greek yogurt
grated zest of 1 orange or lemon
120g caster sugar

Scatter the fruit over the base of a 2-litre oven-to-table dish. Combine the custard, Greek yogurt and grated zest in a bowl and spoon over the fruit. Sprinkle with the caster sugar and set under the grill until bubbling and golden. Alternatively, use a blowtorch. Serve chilled and impress!

Variation
Add a little chopped stem ginger or a dash of Amaretto to the mix.

Brandied Chocolate Mousse ⓟ

This gloriously rich, chocolatey recipe freezes perfectly. It is suitable for Passover if you make it with parve whipping cream. However, it does contain raw egg white.
Serves 12 generous portions

525g fairtrade dark chocolate (70 per cent cocoa solids), plus extra for decoration
3 organic free-range egg whites
115g fairtrade soft dark brown sugar
115g icing sugar
2 x 425ml tubs Kosher Dairy Substitute Whip
75ml brandy

Line 2 x 450g loaf tins or plastic containers with clingfilm.

Melt the chocolate in a heatproof bowl over a saucepan of barely simmering water. Make sure the hot water doesn't come into contact with the bottom of the bowl. Whisk the egg whites in a grease-free bowl until stiff peaks form. Add the sugars and keep whisking until thick and glossy. In a separate bowl, whip the cream until soft peaks form. Add the brandy and whip again. Carefully fold the meringue mixture into the cream, taking care not to knock out any air. Take a spoonful of the creamy meringue and carefully fold it into the melted chocolate to soften it. Pour the chocolate into the bowl with the creamy meringue and fold it in quickly and carefully. Tip into your prepared containers, cover the top with clingfilm and place in the freezer to set.

To serve, turn out the chocolate mousse onto a pretty dish and grate over some chocolate shavings using a vegetable peeler. It can be served from frozen.

Variation
Try replacing the Kosher Dairy Substitute Whip with about 850ml whipping cream or cream substitute.

Easy Delicious Peach Cobbler

 or Ⓜ

The American Jewish community adopted this recipe – a spiced scone topping covering a layer of poached peaches.

Serves 6

6–8 fresh peaches or nectarines
1 x 200g tin peaches in juice
1 tablespoon cornflour
275g self-raising flour
½ teaspoon baking powder
25g fairtrade soft light brown sugar
pinch of salt
10g vanilla sugar
½ teaspoon ground cinnamon (optional)
50g butter (or dairy-free margarine)
85ml milk (or soya milk)
1 organic free-range egg, beaten
grated zest of 1 lemon
a dusting of caster sugar

Preheat the oven to 180°C/gas mark 4. Stone (and peel, if desired) the fresh peaches or nectarines and combine them with the tinned peaches and juice in a glass bowl. Microwave on high for 10 minutes, or until the fruit is just tender. Leave to cool slightly. Strain the peaches through a nylon sieve set over a measuring jug to catch the juice. Blend the cornflour with 2 tablespoons cold water in a separate bowl. Gradually pour in the hot peach juice, whisking all the time to prevent lumps. Pour into a 1.5-litre oven-to-table dish and stir in the cooked peaches.

To make the cobbler topping, sift the self-raising flour and baking powder into a large mixing bowl. Sift in the sugar (brown sugar often has lumps), salt, vanilla sugar and cinnamon (if using). Rub in the butter or margarine with your fingertips to form breadcrumbs. In a measuring jug, combine the milk with half the beaten egg and the lemon zest. Make a well in the centre of the dry ingredients, pour in the milk and egg mixture and combine carefully to form a soft, sticky dough. You may need a little more flour if the mixture is very sticky.

Gently roll out the dough on a floured work surface to about 3–4cm thick, and cut into circles using a 4–5cm fluted cutter. Layer the pastry circles over the peach mixture to form a decorative pattern and brush with the reserved beaten egg. Sprinkle with sugar and bake in the oven for 15–20 minutes or until golden brown.

Chocolate and Orange Dainty Ⓟ

Lemon Dainty was a favourite in my childhood home. In this chocolate variation, soya milk and dairy-free margarine are substituted to make this dessert suitable for a milk or meat meal.

Serves 4–6

50g dairy-free margarine, plus extra for greasing
120g fairtrade soft dark brown sugar
1 vanilla pod
2 organic free-range eggs, separated
50g self-raising flour
175g fairtrade dark chocolate (70 per cent cocoa solids), finely chopped
300ml soya milk
juice and grated zest of 1 orange

Preheat the oven to 180°C/gas mark 4 and grease a 1.2-litre ovenproof dish. Cream the margarine and sugar until light and fluffy. Split the vanilla pod in half, scrape the seeds into the bowl and add the egg yolks, flour, finely chopped chocolate, milk and orange juice and zest. Beat together with a wooden spoon until thoroughly combined – the mixture might curdle but this will not affect the outcome of the pudding. In a separate, grease-free bowl, whisk the egg whites until stiff peaks form. Carefully fold the egg whites into the chocolate mixture, taking care not to knock out any air. Pour the mixture into the prepared dish and set it inside a roasting tin. Fill the roasting tin with boiling water to form a bain-marie, and then carefully transfer it to the oven. Bake for 45–50 minutes until golden and set on the top. Relish a taste of the past.

This dish can be prepared in advance and microwaved to reheat it.

Variation
For a healthier, fruity twist, omit the chocolate and substitute with a punnet of raspberries or blueberries.

8: Cakes & Baking

*'And when thou bringest a meal offering baked in the oven,
it shall be unleavened cakes of fine flour mingled with oil
or unleavened wafers spread with oil'*

LEVITICUS 2:4

Judith's Black and White Cake (P) or (M)

I have a vast cake tin, the family heirloom, carried by my mother when she was a mere child of twelve, as she escaped pre-war Germany. Later she used it to bake a richly moist chocolate and vanilla cake, known affectionately as Black and White Cake.

If you are making the Parve version, be sure to use dairy-free chocolate.

Makes 1 large cake or 2 smaller cakes

200g fairtrade dark chocolate (70 per cent cocoa solids)
350g butter (or dairy-free margarine)
350g fairtrade soft light brown sugar
grated zest of 1 orange
juice of ½ orange
1 teaspoon vanilla extract
5 organic free-range eggs
175g self-raising flour
200g plain flour
2 tablespoons milk (or soya milk)

To decorate
200g fairtrade dark chocolate (70 per cent cocoa solids)
candied orange peel, to decorate (optional)

Preheat the oven to 180°C/gas mark 4 and grease and line your tin(s). I use a large tin, 24cm in diameter and 12cm deep. Alternatively, use 2 x 900g loaf tins. (For one smaller cake, halve the quantities and use 1 x 900g loaf tin or 1 x 25cm bundt tin.)

Melt the chocolate in a heatproof bowl set over a pan of gently simmering water. Leave to cool.

Meanwhile, cream the margarine with the sugar, orange zest and juice and vanilla extract until light and fluffy. Beat in the eggs a little at a time with a spoonful of flour to prevent the mixture curdling. Carefully fold in the remaining flour, along with enough milk to form a dropping consistency. Divide the cake mixture into two separate bowls and fold the melted chocolate into one of the bowls.

To create a marbled effect, drop alternate spoonfuls of chocolate and white cake mixture into your cake tin(s). Drag a skewer through the mixture twice.

Bake in the oven for 50–60 minutes for one large cake, or 30–40 minutes for two smaller cakes.

Remove from the oven and leave to cool completely before drizzling with melted chocolate and topping with candied orange peel (if using).

Shabbat Almond, Peach and Apple Kuchen ⓟ or Ⓜ

This luscious cake was part of my childhood – baked on Friday for the Sabbath when its fragrant yeasty dough and moist apple filling were the star of the meal. Here is the cake with my own variations: the apples are poached with a tin of peaches in their own juice, while ground almonds are added to the filling for a sumptuous taste and texture. It is glorious served hot straight out of the oven with custard, cream or ice-cream and freezes perfectly.

James Martin tasted and enjoyed it in my kitchen, and it has also featured on the *Hairy Bikers: Mums Know Best* website.

Serves 8–10

For the rich yeast dough
150ml lukewarm milk (or soya milk)
2 level teaspoons dried yeast
350g organic strong white bread flour
a pinch of salt
60g butter (or dairy-free margarine)
60g caster sugar, plus 1 teaspoon
10g vanilla sugar
grated zest of ½ orange
grated zest of ½ lemon
2 organic free-range eggs

For the filling
2 large Bramley apples
10g vanilla sugar
1 x 411g tin peaches in juice
125g sultanas
grated zest of ½ orange
grated zest of ½ lemon
a few drops of almond extract
100g ground almonds

To decorate
about 100g icing sugar
juice of ½ lemon
pecan nuts, pumpkin seeds and
   crystallised violets

Pour the warm milk into a small bowl and whisk in the yeast, 1 teaspoon sugar and 1 heaped tablespoon flour. Set aside in a warm place to ferment for about 15 minutes until bubbles appear on the surface.

Meanwhile, prepare the filling. Peel and core the apples, roughly chop the flesh and place in a pan with the vanilla sugar. Strain the peach juice into the pan and set over a medium-low heat. Bring to the boil, put on a lid and simmer gently until the apples are tender and fluffy. Add the drained peaches, sultanas, grated orange and lemon zest and almond extract. Fold in the ground almonds a spoonful at a time to make a soft, but not slopping, filling. You may need to add extra (or less) ground almonds depending on the moisture of your apples. Set aside.

Sift the remaining flour with a pinch of salt into a large mixing bowl. Rub in the butter or margarine with your fingers and stir in the sugars and grated orange and lemon zest. Add one of the eggs to the bubbling yeast mixture and beat well with a fork. Pour the mixture into the dry ingredients and combine to a soft, pliable dough. Turn out onto a floured work surface and knead until smooth. Place the dough back in the bowl, cover with a clean tea towel and leave to rise in a warm place for about 40–60 minutes until doubled in size.

Preheat the oven to 200°C/gas mark 6 and line a large baking sheet with baking parchment. Tip out the dough onto a floured work surface and punch out the air with your fists. Roll out the dough to form a long rectangle, 30 x 16cm. Spread the apple filling over the dough, leaving a border all around, tuck in the ends and then roll up like a Swiss roll. Place on your prepared baking sheet, slash the top a few times diagonally to reveal some of the filling and cover with the same tea towel. Leave to rise in a warm place for about 20–30 minutes until doubled in size.

Glaze the kuchen with the remaining beaten egg and bake in the hot oven for 25–30 minutes until puffed up and golden. Remove from the oven and leave to cool on the tin.

To make the topping, mix the icing sugar with the lemon juice to form a stiff icing. Drizzle over the hot cake and decorate with nuts, seeds and crystallised violets. Serve warm or cold.

Super-moist Yom Tov Peach Dessert Cake (P)

This delicious cake suits any Yom Tov or special Jewish holiday as it has a real luxury feel. The slightly spiced sponge is super-moist from the peaches, with a crunchy streusel topping.

This quantity make two cakes, but they freeze well so it is worth doubling up.

Makes 2 large cakes

For the cake
3 x 200g tins peaches in juice
grated zest and juice of 1 lemon
2 teaspoons vanilla extract
225g sultanas (or other dried fruit)
450g self-raising flour
1 teaspoon mixed spice
1 teaspoon ground cinnamon
300g soft dairy-free margarine
200g fairtrade soft light brown sugar
4 organic free-range eggs

For the streusel topping
25g fairtrade light or dark brown muscovado sugar
75g self-raising flour
25g rolled oats
2 tablespoons light olive oil

Preheat the oven to 160°C/gas mark 3 and line two deep cake tins, 18cm in diameter.

Drain the peaches (saving the juice for stewing fruit) and place in a food-processor with the lemon zest and juice and vanilla extract. Blitz to a smooth purée. Pour into a bowl and combine with the sultanas (or dried fruit of your choice). Set aside for 10–15 minutes to allow the fruit to plump up.

Sift the flour and spices into a bowl and rub in the margarine with your fingers. Stir in the sugar. Add the beaten eggs and fruit purée and combine well. Divide the gloriously soft fragrant mixture between the cake tins and set aside while you make the topping.

To make the topping, combine the sugar, flour, oats and oil in a small bowl. Sprinkle over the cakes and bake in the oven for about 1¼ hours until golden brown on top and shrinking away from the sides of the tin. To check it is cooked, insert a skewer – it should come out clean. Serve warm or cold.

Honey Cake

At the Jewish New Year, Jewish people eat apples dipped in honey and bake honey cake (or lekach), hoping for a good, sweet year to come. And what could be better than this luxurious version – rich with dried fruit, nuts and a dash of brandy – to celebrate a special occasion?

Serves 10–12

225g plain flour
¾ teaspoon bicarbonate of soda
1 teaspoon ground cinnamon
1½–2 teaspoons ground ginger
120g butter (or dairy-free margarine)
80g honey
60g golden syrup
120g fairtrade soft light or dark brown sugar
125g luxury mixed dried fruit
100g chopped pecans or pistachios (optional)
grated zest of 1 lemon
2 organic free-range eggs
4 tablespoons milk (or soya milk)
juice of ½ lemon
2 tablespoons brandy or apple brandy (optional)

Preheat the oven to 170°C/gas mark 3 and line a cake tin, 21cm in diameter.

Sift the flour, bicarbonate of soda and spices into a large mixing bowl. Melt the butter or margarine in a medium pan with the honey, golden syrup and soft brown sugar. Stir in the dried fruit, chopped nuts (if using) and lemon zest and set aside to cool.

In a separate jug, beat the eggs with the milk and lemon juice. Pour into the dried fruit mixture and combine well. Quickly fold in the flour and spices – the bicarbonate of soda will begin to react immediately – to form a smooth batter. Pour into the prepared cake tin and bake in the oven for 1 hour. Avoid opening the oven door while the cake is cooking or it will sink in the middle.

Remove from the oven and leave to cool in the tin for at least 20 minutes before turning out onto a wire rack to cool completely. Once the cake is completely cold, pierce the cake all over with a wooden skewer and carefully pour over the brandy (if using).

Variation
Substitute the dried fruit or nuts with chopped stem ginger.

Easy Carrot, Orange and Olive Oil Cake

Instead of doughnuts, why not bake a healthy cake enriched with olive oil for Chanukah? This one can also be served warm as a dessert.

Serves 10

140g plain flour
¼ teaspoon baking powder
¼ teaspoon bicarbonate of soda
a pinch of salt
5 heaped tablespoons ground nuts – almonds or walnuts are wonderful
2 organic free-range eggs
225g fairtrade light brown muscovado sugar
180ml light olive oil
180ml orange juice (equivalent to about 1½ oranges)
zest of 1½ oranges
juice of ½ lemon
1 teaspoon vanilla extract
300g carrots, peeled and finely grated

For the icing
juice of ½ lemon
150g icing sugar

Preheat the oven to 180°C/gas mark 4 and line a deep cake tin, 23cm in diameter. Sift the flour with the baking powder and bicarbonate of soda into a large mixing bowl. Stir in the salt and ground nuts. Beat the eggs with the sugar in a separate bowl using a handheld mixer. Make a well in the centre of the dry ingredients and add the olive oil, orange juice, orange zest, lemon juice and vanilla. Add the egg and sugar mixture and quickly mix to a smooth batter. Finally, fold in the grated carrots. Spoon into the prepared cake tin and bake in the oven for 40–50 minutes. To test if it is cooked, insert a skewer in the centre – it should come out clean. Let the cake cool in the tin for 20 minutes, and then turn out onto a wire rack to cool completely.

To make the icing, combine the lemon juice with the icing sugar, mix to a smooth, runny paste and drizzle over the cake.

This cake will last for a few days if kept in a cool place. It also freezes well.

Variation
For an aromatic version, add the crushed seeds of 3 cardamom pods (discard the husks).

Apple Cake

This apple cake is part of Jewish baking history. Although shop-bought versions are available, they'll never beat homemade. Serve hot or cold as a dessert with custard or ice-cream, or simply with good coffee and a schmooze.

Serves 4–5

170g butter or dairy-free margarine
grated zest of 1 lemon
120g fairtrade soft light brown sugar
1 organic free-range egg
270g self-raising flour
a pinch of salt
4 tablespoons apricot jam or marmalade
450g Bramley cooking apples, or Jonagold for a sweeter flavour
juice of ½ lemon
15g vanilla sugar
1½ tablespoons custard powder (or cornflour)
egg yolk, to glaze
2 tablespoons caster sugar
icing sugar, to dust

Preheat the oven to 170°C/gas mark 3 and grease and flour a springform cake tin 18cm in diameter.

Cream the butter or margarine with the lemon zest, sugar and egg. Fold in the flour and salt. (The mixture will seem quite stiff.) Spread three-quarters of the cake mixture over the base of your prepared cake tin, using the back of a spoon to spread it into the corners and slightly up the sides. Warm the jam or marmalade and spread over the top.

Peel the apples and cut into thin slices. Place them in a bowl and squeeze over the lemon juice. Add the vanilla sugar and the custard powder or cornflour and stir gently until they are evenly coated in the lemon and sugar. Carefully arrange the apples over the cake mixture in overlapping circles.

To create the lattice pattern on top, remove handfuls of the remaining cake mixture using slightly wet hands and roll into long strips. Decorate the top of the cake in a lattice pattern. Beat the egg yolk with a little water to create an eggwash and brush over the top. Sprinkle with caster sugar. Bake in the oven for 1 hour until golden brown. Remove from the oven and dust with icing sugar while still hot.

Simcha Fruit Cake

 or Ⓜ

This has to be the simplest, moistest cake in the world. The secret lies in the overnight soaking of the fruit.

Serves 15–20

750g mixed dried fruit – such as sultanas, raisins or currants
100g glacé cherries, halved
100g chopped dates
100g chopped apricots
1 small can of beer, about 330ml (or mango juice)
2 tablespoons mixed spice
2 tablespoons marmalade
1 tablespoon golden syrup
zest and juice of 1 lemon
350g butter or dairy-free margarine
350g fairtrade dark brown muscovado sugar
1 teaspoon vanilla extract
¼ teaspoon almond extract
6 organic free-range eggs, beaten
100g self-raising flour
250g plain flour
3–4 tablespoons brandy (optional)

Place the dried fruit in a large bowl, pour over the beer, add the mixed spice, marmalade, golden syrup and lemon zest and juice, and stir well to combine. Cover with a tea towel and leave to soak for at least 8 hours (preferably overnight).

Preheat the oven to 170°C/gas mark 3 and line a deep tin, 23cm in diameter, with baking parchment.

Cream the margarine or butter with the sugar, vanilla and almond extract until light and fluffy. Beat in the eggs a little at a time, along with a tablespoon of the flour to stop the mixture curdling. Carefully fold in the rest of the flour. Tip in the soaked fruit and mix well to combine. Spoon the mixture into your prepared tin and smooth the top. Bake in the oven for 1½–2 hours. If necessary, lower the temperature after the first hour if the cake seems to be browning too quickly. Remove from the oven and leave to cool in the tin. A day or so later, pierce the cake all over with a wooden skewer and pour over the brandy (if using). Wrap in foil until needed.

This cake looks glorious decorated with dried fruit and glazed with marmalade or apricot jam. Finish with a large bow to cover the sides.

Baked Lemon Cheesecake for Shavuot

This featherlight baked lemon cheesecake may crack slightly as it cools, but that adds to its charm. To serve, arrange some of your favourite soft fruit on top and cut into generous slices.

Serves 12

For the biscuit crust
220g digestive or gingernut biscuits
50g margarine or butter

For the cheese filling
3 organic free-range eggs
500g cream cheese
15g vanilla sugar
1 tablespoon caster sugar
zest of 1 lemon
300ml whipping cream
1 tablespoon custard powder

For the topping
300ml soured cream
1–2 punnets (200–300g) soft fruit of your choice
icing sugar, to dust

Preheat the oven to 170°C/gas mark 3 and grease and flour a springform cake tin 23cm in diameter. To prepare the base, place the biscuits in a plastic bag and crush with a rolling pin. Melt the margarine or butter in a small pan, tip in the crushed biscuits and mix well. Press the mixture into the base of your prepared cake tin and bake for 15 minutes. Set aside to cool slightly.

Separate the eggs and place the egg yolks in a large mixing bowl with the cream cheese, sugars and lemon zest. Using a handheld mixer, beat well until thick and creamy. Add the whipping cream and continue beating until glorious soft peaks form. Sift the custard powder into the bowl and fold in gently. In a separate bowl, whisk the egg whites until stiff. Fold a spoonful of the egg whites into the cream cheese mixture to soften it, and then fold in the rest. Spoon the mixture over the biscuit base and smooth the top with a palette knife. Bake for 1 hour 45 minutes. Now open the oven door and carefully spread the soured cream over the surface. Close the door and continue cooking for a further 15 minutes. Switch off the oven and leave the cheesecake to cool in the oven.

Once the cheesecake is completely cold, unclip the sides of the tin and carefully transfer the cake to a serving plate. To serve, decorate with fresh fruit and dust with icing sugar.

Poppy Seed Twist Cake Ⓜ

There are numerous variations of this traditional yeasted poppy seed kuchen, also known as makosh, which originated in Eastern Europe. Before the arrival of the electric spice grinder, grinding the mohn (poppy seeds in German) was always a palaver, but now the process is far easier. The addition of cooked and processed lemon is my own twist, but it combines perfectly with the sweet poppy seed mixture. This would be a perfect cake to make over two days. My cousins make a chocolate version, which seems to be more popular with children.

This recipe makes enough mohn for the makosh and another dessert. As the preparation is quite complicated, either freeze half for another time, halve the quantity or use the remaining mohn to make a simple Mohn Streusel Cake. To do this, roll out 500g of shortcrust pastry onto a 23cm x 21cm Swiss roll tin lined with parchment paper. Spread with about 180g of a sharpish-flavour jam, such as blackcurrant or even marmalade. Top with the mohn filling and a streusel topping (see page 160) and bake for 40 minutes at 180°C/gas mark 4. Delicious warm or cold.

Serves 10–12

For the rich yeast dough
2 teaspoons dried yeast
150ml lukewarm milk
350g organic strong white bread flour
a pinch of salt
60g caster sugar, plus 1 teaspoon
10g vanilla sugar
zest of ½ orange
zest of ½ lemon
60g margarine or butter
1 organic free-range egg
icing sugar, for dusting

For the poppy seed filling (mohn)
1 lemon
110g poppy seeds
225ml water or milk
60g margarine or butter
a pinch of salt
1 tablespoon golden syrup
1 tablespoon honey
100g raisins
juice of ½ lemon
200g ground almonds
1 organic free-range egg, beaten,
    to glaze

In a small bowl, whisk the yeast with the warm milk, 1 tablespoon of the flour and 1 teaspoon sugar. Set aside in a warm place to ferment for 20 minutes, or until bubbles appear on the surface.

Sift the remaining flour into a large mixing bowl and stir in the salt, sugars and lemon and orange zest. Melt the butter or margarine and combine with the bubbling yeast mixture. Add the egg and beat well with a fork. Pour into the bowl with the flour and mix to a soft, pliable dough. Turn out onto a floured work surface and knead until smooth.

Place the dough in an oiled bowl, cover with clingfilm or a clean tea towel and set aside to rise in a warm place for 40–60 minutes until doubled in size. Alternatively, leave the dough to rise in the fridge overnight, which will improve the flavour.

Preheat the oven to 190°C/gas mark 5 and grease and flour a 25cm bundt tin. Place the whole lemon in a pan of water and simmer gently for 20 minutes until tender (or place in a bowl of water and microwave for 5 minutes). Cool under cold running water, cut open and remove the pips. Place the lemon (skin and all) into a food-processor and blitz to a smooth pulp.

Grind the poppy seeds until smooth. In a heavy saucepan, combine the water or milk, butter or margarine, salt, golden syrup, honey, raisins, processed lemon and lemon juice and poppy seeds. Simmer gently for about 10 minutes until the mixture thickens slightly. Leave to cool. Carefully fold in the ground almonds.

Turn out the dough onto a floured work surface and roll out as thin as possible to form a rectangle, 31 x 23cm. Spread the poppy seed mixture over the dough and roll up like a Swiss roll, pinching the edges together. Now twist the roll, if possible a couple of times, and lay carefully in the prepared tin. Cover with a clean tea towel and leave to prove in a warm place for 25 minutes until doubled in size.

Glaze with the beaten egg and bake in the oven for about 30 minutes, or until richly golden. Leave to cool in the tin before turning out onto a wire rack to cool completely.

Etrog Drizzle Cake

'And you shall take on the 1st day the fruit of beautiful trees, branches of palm trees and boughs of leafy trees and willows of the brook, and you shall rejoice before the Lord your God 7 days!' Leviticus 23:40

This wonderful take on lemon drizzle cake solves the problem of what do with your fragrant etrog after Succoth.

The etrog – a particular type of lemon-like citrus fruit, otherwise known as a citron – is considered the most beautiful fruit in Jewish understanding, and for this reason it is used in the Succoth service. After the festival has passed, the fruits are no longer needed. So my late mother would collect the community's etrogim, make marmalade and return the fruits to the people, now beautifully fragrant and golden in a jar.

Serves 8

175g self-raising flour
1 teaspoon baking powder
a pinch of salt
175g margarine or butter
175g fairtrade light brown muscovado sugar
10g vanilla sugar
zest of 1 etrog
3 large organic free-range eggs

For the icing
125g fairtrade granulated sugar
60ml etrog juice (if necessary, make up the quantity with grapefruit, orange or lemon juice)

Preheat the oven to 180°C/gas mark 4 and line a deep cake tin, 18cm in diameter. Sift the flour and baking powder into a bowl and add the salt. In a large mixing bowl, cream the margarine or butter with the sugars and etrog zest until light and fluffy. Beat in the eggs, adding a tablespoon of the flour to stop the mixture curdling. Fold in the remaining flour and mix to a smooth batter. Pour into your prepared tin and bake in the oven for about 45–50 minutes. To check it is cooked, insert a skewer – it should come out clean. Leave to cool in the tin.

To make the drizzle topping, combine the sugar with the etrog juice. Use a wooden skewer to make fine holes in the top of the cake and pour over the drizzle topping. Delicious!

Hamantaschen for Purim (P) or (M)

It is intriguing how the Jewish religion weaves symbolic mysticism with food. Hamantaschen are triangular cakes filled with a poppy seed filling. *Mohntaschen* in German comes from the word *mohn*, meaning 'poppy seeds', and *taschen*, meaning 'pockets'. Combine this with the story of wicked Haman – who plotted to annihilate the Jewish race – and we have Hamantaschen or Haman's pockets, supposedly stuffed with bribe money. In Israel, Hamantaschen are called 'Oznei Haman', or 'Haman's ears', describing Haman's punishment of clipped ears. The cake's triangular shape is said to resemble Haman's three-cornered hat. Alfred J Kolatch, in *The Jewish Book of Why*, suggests that the three corners also represent the three patriarchs – Abraham, Isaac and Jacob – who protected Queen Esther and gave her strength. Why poppy seeds? These are the seeds that Esther chose to eat as part of her vegetarian diet in a stranger's traif (non-kosher) court.

Traditionally, the filling in Hamantaschen is the mohn filling in Makosh cake. But not all people enjoy mohn. The simple filling I've given here is more popular with children. It takes seconds to prepare and is easy on the teeth! The recipe can be made in one afternoon or spread out over two days.

Makes 18

150ml lukewarm milk (or soya milk)
2 teaspoons dried yeast
350g organic strong white bread flour
2 teaspoons vanilla sugar
grated zest of 1 orange
grated zest of 1 lemon
a pinch of salt
50g butter (or dairy-free margarine)
50g fairtrade soft light brown sugar
2 organic free-range eggs

For the filling
½ jar (about 180g) good-quality jam – apricot, black cherry or strawberry
1 tablespoon lemon juice
150g ground almonds
a few drops of almond extract

In a small bowl, whisk the warm milk with the yeast, 2 tablespoons flour, the vanilla sugar and the grated lemon and orange zest. Set aside to ferment in a warm place until bubbles appear on the surface.

Sift the remaining flour and salt into a large bowl and rub in the butter or margarine with your fingers (or use a mixer). Stir in the brown sugar. Add one of the eggs to the bubbling yeast mixture and beat well with a fork. Pour the yeast mixture into the flour mixture and combine to a soft, pliable dough. Turn out onto a floured work surface and knead until smooth. Place the dough in a clean, oiled bowl, cover with clingfilm or a clean tea towel and set aside to rise in a warm place for about 1 hour, or until doubled in size. Alternatively, leave the dough to rise in the fridge overnight, which will improve the flavour.

Preheat the oven to 200°C/gas mark 6 and line two baking sheets with baking parchment. To prepare the filling, scoop the jam into a bowl and mix with the lemon juice, ground almonds and almond extract.

To make the Hamantaschen, shape the dough into balls roughly the size of a golf ball and roll out to flat circles, 12cm in diameter. Place a teaspoon of the filling in the centre of each circle. Bring up the sides to form a triangle and pinch together at the three corners. Arrange the Hamantaschen on the prepared baking sheets, cover with a tea towel and leave to prove in a warm place for 20–30 minutes until nicely puffed up. Beat the remaining egg to form an eggwash and brush over the Hamantaschen to glaze. Bake in the oven for 25–30 minutes until golden. Serve hot or cold and celebrate a symbolic Purim.

These freeze really well and can be reheated in a low oven.

Rich Fruit and
Cheese Roll

This is a typical Ashkenazi recipe, made with cream and curd cheese to celebrate Shavuot. The rolled effect resembles a strudel, but the cheese in this pastry makes for an altogether richer dish.

Serves 8

For the pastry
120g plain flour
50g self-raising flour
120g butter
2 tablespoons icing sugar
120g curd cheese
zest of 1 lemon

For the filling
240g curd cheese
zest of 1 lemon
110g raisins or sultanas
60g fairtrade soft light brown sugar

To glaze
1 organic free-range egg, beaten
a little caster sugar, for dusting

Preheat the oven to 200°C/gas mark 6 and line a baking sheet with baking parchment. To make the pastry, sift the flours into a large mixing bowl and rub in the butter with your fingers. Sift in the icing sugar and add the curd cheese and lemon zest. Mix to a soft, sticky dough and form into a ball. Wrap in clingfilm and chill in the fridge for 30 minutes.

Meanwhile, combine all the ingredients for the filling in a bowl.

Roll out the pastry to form a rectangle, 23 x 21cm. Spread the filling over the pastry and roll up like a strudel, tucking in the ends. Place on your prepared baking sheet, glaze with beaten egg and dust lightly with caster sugar. Bake in the oven for 15 minutes, and then reduce the temperature to 180°C/gas mark 4 and bake for a further 15 minutes. Serve warm with coffee.

Doughnuts for Chanukah

The tradition of eating fried foods symbolises the miracle of Chanukah, when the holy oil in the Temple was ravaged by soldiers and one day's oil lasted for eight days. Celebrate the joy of this occasion with doughnuts. Choose from the traditional yeast method (below) or the magic cheat's version opposite.

Makes 12

10g dried yeast
2½ tablespoons vanilla sugar
530g plain flour
2 tablespoons warm water
½ teaspoon salt
35g margarine or butter
1 organic free-range egg
300ml warm milk
vegetable oil, for deep-frying
caster sugar, for rolling

In a small bowl, whisk together the yeast, vanilla sugar, 1 tablespoon of the flour and the warm water. Set aside in a warm place to ferment for 20 minutes until bubbles appear on the surface.

Sift the remaining flour into a large mixing bowl, add the salt and rub in the butter or margarine with your fingers. Stir in the remaining vanilla sugar. Crack the egg into a glass and, after checking for any blood spots, add to the bubbling yeast mixture and beat well with a fork. Make a well in the centre of the dry ingredients and pour in the yeast mixture along with enough warm milk to mix to a soft dough. Tip onto a floured work surface and knead for 5 minutes until smooth. Place the dough in an oiled bowl, cover with clingfilm or a clean tea towel and set aside to rise in a warm place for 1 hour until doubled in size, or in the fridge overnight.

Shape the dough into 12 balls and set on a baking sheet lined with parchment paper. (Alternatively, roll out the dough with a rolling pin and cut with large cutters and follow with smaller cutters to make ring doughnuts and tiny round doughnut shapes.) Cover with a clean tea towel and leave to prove in a warm place for 40–50 minutes until swollen and puffy.

Preheat the oil in a deep-fat fryer to 190°C and fry the doughnuts for 3–4 minutes on each side until golden brown – you might have to do this in batches. Drain on kitchen paper and roll in caster sugar while still hot.

Magic Cheat's Doughnuts ⓜ

Makes 6

6 slices of stale white bread
6 generous tablespoons jam of your choice
1 organic free-range egg, beaten
40ml milk
a few drops of vanilla extract
vegetable oil, for shallow-frying
caster sugar, for dusting

Place the slices of bread on a work surface and cut out 12 circles, 4.5cm in diameter, with a fluted cutter. Place a generous teaspoon of jam in the centre of each and brush the edges with a little beaten egg. Take pairs of circles and press one on top of the other, pinching the edges together all the way round to prevent the jam escaping. Beat any remaining egg with the milk and vanilla extract in a small bowl. Heat the oil in a frying pan until it is smoking hot. Dip the 'doughnuts' in the egg mixture and fry until golden on both sides. Remove from the pan, dust with sugar and serve hot.

BISCUITS

Schmoozing and noshing – what better way than with a glass of tea and a homemade biscuit? Enjoy.

Vanilla and Almond Kipferl

These fragrant, half-moon-shaped biscuits were part of my mother's repertoire for special occasions. Easy to produce, they look professional when finished. Sometimes she'd dip the ends in bitter chocolate.

Makes 30 (double up for a party – they disappear!)

110g margarine (I use cholesterol-lowering spread) or butter
20g caster sugar
20g vanilla sugar
60g icing sugar
½ teaspoon vanilla extract
120g plain flour
70g ground almonds
icing sugar, to dust

Preheat the oven to 150°C/gas mark 2 and line two baking sheets with baking parchment. Cream the margarine with the sugars until light and fluffy. Add the vanilla extract, flour and almonds and combine to a soft dough. Wrap in clingfilm and chill in the fridge for 30 minutes.

Roll the dough into walnut-sized balls, and then roll each ball out to form a sausage shape 5cm long. Curve the ends to make a horseshoe shape and arrange on your prepared baking sheets.

Bake in the oven for 40–60 minutes, or until firm but not coloured. Transfer to a wire rack to cool, and then dust with icing sugar.

Variation

Flavour the biscuit dough with a few drops of almond extract or some grated lemon or orange zest. For a completely different flavour, substitute the ground almonds for ground hazelnuts or walnuts.

Stuffed Monkeys

 or

I have never understood why these biscuits are called stuffed monkeys. Perhaps it's the spicy brown crust that gives the impression of monkey fur? Whatever the reason, the flavour is wonderful. You could also use the dough as an unusual pastry alternative in a fruit tart.

Makes 20 squares but can also be served whole

For the dough
160g self-raising flour
1 teaspoon ground cinnamon
1 teaspoon mixed spice
a pinch of salt
75g butter (or dairy-free margarine)
60g fairtrade soft dark brown sugar
1 organic free-range egg, beaten
a squeeze of lemon juice

For the filling
65g ground hazelnuts or walnuts
½ jar (180ml) of thick-cut marmalade
150g mixed peel
a pinch of salt

Preheat the oven to 180°C/gas mark 4 and grease and line a 20cm square tin. To make the pastry, sift the flour with the spices into a bowl and stir in the salt. Rub in the margarine with your fingers and stir in the brown sugar. Add half of the beaten egg, along with the lemon juice and mix to a soft dough. Wrap in clingfilm and leave to rest in the fridge for 30 minutes.

To make the filling, place the rest of the beaten egg in a bowl and stir in the ground nuts. Add the marmalade, mixed peel and salt and combine well.

Cut the pastry in half and roll out one piece to fit the base of your tin – or simply press it into the tin with your fingers. Spread the filling evenly over the pastry. Top with the remaining piece of pastry – either roll out, as before, or grate it over the top to give a crumbled texture. Bake in the oven for 40–50 minutes until fragrant and golden. Cut into squares while still warm, then leave to cool so the mixture sets perfectly.

Variation
For an alternative filling, combine 130g dried cranberries, 65g ground almonds and ½ egg.

Mandelbrot

Gertie, my dear late mother-in-law, used to serve these up alongside a cup of tea. Brewed by Dad, and deep mahogany in colour, it was so strong 'a mouse could trot across it' – as the Welsh saying goes.

These traditional biscuits, with their sweet, melting flavour, are made to dunk! I'm honoured to use her recipe, although I have adapted it slightly with soft brown sugar to give a more intense flavour. The pistachios lend a glorious colour and professional-looking result. Enjoy.

Makes 40

100g shelled pistachios
700g plain flour
2 heaped teaspoons baking powder
4 organic free-range eggs
275ml light vegetable oil
4 teaspoons vanilla sugar
170g fairtrade soft light brown sugar
1 teaspoon vanilla extract
½ teaspoon almond extract
grated zest of 1 orange
1 teaspoon mixed spice or ground cinnamon
100g flaked almonds

Preheat the oven to 180°C/gas mark 4 and line two baking sheets with parchment paper. Pulse or roughly chop the pistachios so that they end up the size of chocolate chips (not a paste). Sift the flour with the baking powder and set aside. In a mixer, whisk the eggs with the oil and sugars until light and frothy. Add the rest of the ingredients and combine to a soft, pliable dough. Wrap in clingfilm and leave to rest in the fridge for 30 minutes.

Divide the dough into 4 pieces and roll out into sausage shapes, 9cm in diameter. Transfer to your baking sheets, allowing plenty of space in between for them to spread. Bake in the oven for 20–25 minutes, or until they are beginning to crack and just starting to colour. Remove from the oven and turn down the temperature to 170°C/gas mark 3.

Using a sharp knife, cut each piece into slices 2cm thick and spread out on the baking sheets. Return to the oven and bake for a further 15 minutes until golden and crisp.

Variations
Substitute orange zest for the lemon zest, omit the nuts and use chocolate chips or candied peel instead.

Fig Rolls

Although these are not strictly a Jewish recipe, they are so much part of my children's childhood that it seemed a shame to omit them.

Makes 65 dainty rolls – it's worth the effort to make lots

For the filling
450g dried figs (stalks removed), finely chopped
1 vanilla pod, de-seeded (add seeds to fig mixture)
juice of ½ lemon

250g butter (or dairy-free margarine)
170g icing sugar
grated zest of 1 lemon
2 organic free-range eggs, beaten
550g plain flour

Line two baking sheets with baking parchment.

Place the fig filling ingredients with 450ml water in a pan and simmer over a low heat until tender, about 10–12 minutes. Pour into a food-processor and blend to a thick paste.

In a bowl, cream the margarine, sugar and lemon zest until lemon and fluffy. Beat in the beaten egg, reserving 2 tablespoons. Fold in the flour to form a soft dough. Wrap the dough in clingfilm and chill in the fridge for at least 30 minutes.

Preheat the oven to 180°C/gas mark 4. On a floured surface, roll out the pastry to a thickness of about 1–1.5cm and cut into 30 x 6cm rectangles. Spread the fig mixture thickly down the centre of each rectangle. Roll lengthways like a Swiss roll, then cut across into bite-sized pieces about 2.5cm wide.

Lay on the prepared baking sheets and brush with the remaining egg. Bake for 30 minutes until golden.

Kichlach P or M

When you need to produce something that looks and tastes homemade, without hours of preparation, these glorious little kichlach take the biscuit. They're perfect to make with children and the results are lusciously mouth-watering.

If you are making the Parve version, be sure to use dairy-free chocolate.

Makes 38

450g self-raising flour
225g butter (or dairy-free margarine)
grated zest of 1 lemon
100g fairtrade soft light brown sugar
1 teaspoon vanilla sugar
3 organic free-range eggs

To decorate
chopped glacé cherries, chopped crystallised ginger, chocolate drops and caster sugar, for rolling

Preheat the oven to 220°C/gas mark 7 and line two baking sheets with baking parchment. Using either a food-processor or mixer, process or cream all the ingredients to form a soft dough. Don't overwork.

Place the chopped glacé cherries, chopped crystallised ginger, chocolate drops and caster sugar on four separate saucers.

Roll the dough into walnut-sized balls, and then roll in the topping of your choice. Arrange on the prepared baking sheets, placing them slightly apart. Bake in the oven for 10 minutes, and then turn down the temperature to 200°C/gas mark 6 and bake for a further 10 minutes. Mmm, try to resist!

The biscuit dough freezes really well. Why not bake half and freeze half for another time?

Sarah Nathan's Chocolate and Almond Biscuits

P or M

Jewish traditions continue and so I proudly present this recipe, created by my daughter Sarah, which my grandchildren Jasmine and Phoebe help to make and adore.

If you are making the Parve version, be sure to use dairy-free chocolate.

Makes 30

230g butter (or dairy-free margarine)0
170g golden caster sugar
1 large organic free-range egg
200g plain flour
60g cocoa powder
60g ground almonds
a few drops of almond extract
170g chocolate chips (white, dark or milk), chopped almonds or chocolate raisins

To decorate
toasted flaked almonds or chocolate buttons

Preheat the oven to 180°C/gas mark 4 and line two baking sheets with baking parchment. Place the margarine or butter in a mixing bowl with the sugar and beat until light and creamy. Add the egg and beat well. Add the flour, cocoa, ground almonds and almond extract, along with the chocolate chips, chopped almonds or chocolate raisins. Combine carefully until the mixture comes together in a ball. (If it is very sticky, add an extra tablespoon of flour; if it is very dry and crumbly, stir in a splash of milk or water.) Wrap in clingfilm and chill in the fridge for 30 minutes.

Roll the mixture into walnut-sized balls and arrange on the baking sheets, spacing them apart to allow room for them to spread. Flatten the tops slightly and decorate with flaked almonds or chocolate buttons. Bake in the oven for 15–20 minutes until starting to crisp up around the outside, but still soft in the middle. Remove from the oven and transfer to a wire rack to cool. (The biscuits will crisp up more as they cool.)

Store in an airtight container for up to a week – if they last that long!

Variation
For those with nut allergies, replace the ground almonds with extra flour and use vanilla extract instead of almond extract.

9: Bread

'He causeth the grass to grow for the cattle, and herb for the service of man; that he may bring forth food out of the earth; and wine that maketh glad the heart of man, and oil to make his face to shine, and bread which strengthens man's heart' Psalm 104:14

Bread has been created since the dawn of civilisation, when a new balmier climate encouraged people to abandon their old hunter-gatherer ways and look to settling and planting crops. It was the Egyptians who came across the magical ability to make bread rise, as a side effect of their beer invention. The resulting air-bound yeasts present caused an accidental fermentation. After this discovery, a starter or barm was used. This early form of yeast was created by mixing a small amount of flour with water, and sometimes dried fruit or honey, and leaving it to ferment for a few days – during which time it was regularly topped up with water or new flour. This has evolved as the basis of artisan bread manufacture today.

Isaiah, chapter 28, describes the sowing of wheat, barley and spelt 'in its field'. And continues: 'Grain must be ground to make bread,' showing the importance of grain in the biblical diet. It was the women who organised the bread-making process – removing the wheat from the chaff, grinding the grains on a special grindstone and baking the bread into loaves. In grander houses and palaces, baking was arranged and carried out by court bakers. In the Temple, specially appointed bakers formed the 'Lechem Hapanim' or Bread of the Presence – and were responsible for placing the loaves on a specially designated table. The loaves were arranged in two rows to offer to G-d and each loaf contained two omers (measures) of flour. Small cups of frankincense were arranged on top of each loaf. These holy loaves were left for a week before being replaced with fresh loaves the following week.

A vital element of the Passover's story describes the Jews' flight from Pharaoh's slavery. In their haste to depart they were forced to place the unrisen dough for their daily bread on their backs because they didn't have sufficient time for it to rise. It is for this reason that Jews eat commemorative matzo or forms of unleavened bread as part of the Passover ritual – always grateful, remembering their exodus from Egypt's slavery.

Pitta Bread

These luscious Middle-Eastern breads are the perfect foil for falafel and hummus. Serve them warm with dips and salads for an instant party atmosphere. Once you have tried this recipe – fragrant with sesame and Kalonji seeds – you will never buy pitta bread again. But if you are nervous of trying this nutty new taste, you could always substitute them for poppy seeds for a more familiar flavour.

Makes 40

700ml warm water
20g dried yeast
1kg plain flour, plus 50g for proving mixture
2 teaspoons fairtrade soft light brown sugar
3 teaspoons salt
5 tablespoons sesame seeds
5 tablespoons Kalonji or nigella seeds
2 tablespoons light olive oil

Place the water, yeast, 2 tablespoons of the flour and the sugar in a bowl and whisk until smooth. Set aside to prove in a warm place for about 20 minutes, or until bubbles appear on the surface.

Combine the remaining flour with the salt and seeds in a large mixing bowl – I use my mixer with the dough hook attached. Pour in the yeast mixture and mix to a soft, pliable dough. Knead well for at least 10 minutes. Transfer the dough to a clean, oiled bowl, cover with oiled clingfilm and leave to rise in a warm place for about 1 hour until doubled in size.

Preheat the oven to 230°C/gas mark 8 and line two baking sheets with baking parchment. If you have a baking stone, place it in the oven now to heat up. Tip out the dough onto a floured work surface and divide into 40 golfball-sized pieces. Roll each one into a ball and then flatten them out to a circle about 1.5cm thick. Set aside on your prepared baking sheets, cover with a clean cloth and leave to prove in a warm place for about 20 minutes, or until puffed up.

Carefully transfer the pitta breads, 3 or 4 at a time, onto your baking sheets or baking stone. If you don't have a baking stone, you can simply lay them directly on the middle rack inside the oven, placing another rack on top to give a lovely crisscross pattern. Bake for 5 minutes until brown spots appear on the surface, and then turn them over and cook them for a further 3–4 minutes on the other side until puffed up all over. Remove them from the oven and keep warm under a clean tea towel while you cook the rest.

Pretzels – the Catholic bread
that became a Jewish speciality ⓟ

Some time between the 5th and 7th centuries, a monk was playing with leftover bread dough by twisting pencil-sized rolls into an elaborate shape that looked like a person's arms folded in prayer. Gradually these 'pretiola' (literally 'little prayer') breads were used as an integral part of church life. They became part of the marriage ceremony, where the bride and groom would tug on a pretzel – like a wishbone – establishing the expression 'tying the knot'.

The Jewish pretzel influence probably came with the migration of the Jews from Eastern Europe to America, since during the Depression numerous pretzel vendors were seen on the streets of the Lower East Side. Certainly the manufacturing process, whereby the dough is immersed in hot liquid, is very similar to their doughy cousin, the bagel. The difference lies in the immersion bath – which in this case is a lye bath with a good sprinkling of salt on top of the glaze.

It's not possible to buy lye, so I suggest you dissolve a little baking powder in the water as a substitute to give some of that glorious pretzel flavour. The recipe is delicious and worthwhile making. It just takes a little patience because the dough is prepared on one day, left overnight in the fridge, and then formed, dipped and baked the next. However, the results are fabulous. Traditionally, some pretzels are brushed with melted butter before baking but to keep them parve, this process has been omitted.

For the dough
575g organic strong white bread flour
4 tablespoons fairtrade soft light brown
  sugar
2 teaspoons salt
1 tablespoon dried yeast

For the cooking liquid
3 tablespoons baking powder

For the glaze
rock salt for decoration and extra flavour
1 organic free-range egg,
  beaten with a little oil
sesame seeds, poppy seeds, nigella seeds,
  onion seeds, or even soft cooked onion

Combine the ingredients for the dough with 445ml hand-hot water in a food-processor or mixer. Tip out onto a floured work surface and knead for at least 5 minutes. Place the dough in an oiled bowl, cover with oiled clingfilm and leave to rise in the fridge for 24 hours.

The following day, preheat the oven to 220°C/gas mark 7, line two baking sheets with baking parchment and sprinkle with flour. Tip out the dough onto a floured work surface and divide into 12 balls. Roll out each ball to form a rope the same width as a pencil. Shape the rope into a rough 'heart' shape with the tails hanging down in the centre. Twist the tails together to form a 'waist' in the middle and then flatten the tips of the tails and press them down on either side of the 'heart'. Dip the base of each pretzel in flour and place on your floured baking sheets. Cover with a clean cloth and leave to prove in a warm place for 30 minutes. Meanwhile, crush the rock salt in a mortar and pestle.

Preheat the oven to 220°C/gas mark 7. Bring 450ml water to the boil in a wide, deep frying pan and whisk in the baking powder. To cook the pretzels, carefully lower them about three at a time into the boiling water with a slotted spoon and count to 12. Remove them from the pan and return them to the parchment paper. Glaze with the beaten egg mixed with a little oil and sprinkle with seeds or onion. Bake in the hot oven for about 20 minutes until golden brown. Serve hot or cold and enjoy, revelling in your family and friends' praises.

Easy Caraway Rye (P)

This quick recipe tastes like it has taken hours to prepare. It is worth buying the best flour for a better flavour.

Makes 15 rolls

500g whole rye flour
500g organic strong white bread flour
1 teaspoon salt
4 tablespoons caraway seeds, plus extra for sprinkling
2 tablespoons dried yeast
2 tablespoons black molasses
4 tablespoons light olive oil
1 organic free-range egg, beaten, for glazing

Place the flours in a large mixing bowl with the salt and caraway seeds. In small bowl, mix together the yeast with the molasses and 600ml lukewarm water. Whisk in 1 tablespoon of the flour and set aside to ferment in a warm place for about 15 minutes, or until bubbles appear on the surface. Add the oil and beat with a fork until smooth.

Line two baking sheets with baking parchment. Pour the yeast mixture into the dry ingredients and mix to a very soft dough. If necessary, you may need to add a little more tepid water. Place the dough in a clean bowl, cover with a clean cloth or clingfilm and leave to rise in a warm place for about 30 minutes or until doubled in size.

Tip out the dough onto a floured work surface and shape into 15 generous rolls. Place on your prepared baking sheets, cover with a cloth or oiled clingfilm and leave to prove for 30 minutes.

Preheat the oven to 210°C/gas mark 6½. When the rolls are risen, glaze with the beaten egg and sprinkle with more caraway seeds. Bake in the hot oven for about 15–20 minutes until golden brown. You will know when the rolls are cooked because they will sound hollow when you tap them on the base. Glorious!

Granary Bread

This granary bread recipe, first published in *Olive* magazine, was created for my husband as a healthy addition to his lunch.

Makes 2 loaves or 25 rolls

2 teaspoons black molasses
25g dried yeast
700g granary flour
225g organic strong white bread flour
1 teaspoons salt
100g mixed sunflower seeds, pumpkin seeds and whole roasted cashew nuts
25g caraway seeds
225g whole porridge oats
50ml olive oil
beaten organic free-range egg, to glaze
sesame seeds or sunflower seeds, for the topping

Combine the molasses with 700ml warm water, yeast and 2 tablespoons flour in a bowl. Set aside in a warm place to ferment for 15 minutes.

Combine the remaining flours in a large bowl and stir in the salt, seeds, nuts and oats.

Add the olive oil to the molasses mixture and beat with a fork until smooth. Pour the molasses mixture in the dry ingredients and combine to a soft, sticky dough. You may need to add a little more flour or water, as necessary, depending on the dryness of the mixture. Turn out onto a floured work surface and knead for 10 minutes until smooth. Place the dough in an oiled bowl, cover with clingfilm and leave to rise in a warm place for 1 hour, or until doubled in size.

Preheat the oven to 200°C/gas mark 6 and grease 2 x 900g loaf tins. Tip out the dough onto a floured work surface and knock back with your fists. Shape into 2 loaves and place in the prepared tins. Alternatively, shape into 25 rolls and set on two baking sheets lined with baking parchment. Cover the loaves or rolls with a clean cloth and leave to prove in a warm place for 30 minutes until doubled in size. Glaze with beaten egg and sprinkle the seeds on top. Bake the loaves for about 40 minutes until golden; bake the rolls for about 20–25 minutes. You can tell when the bread is cooked because it will sound hollow when you tap it on the base.

Variation
For fig and walnut bread: substitute 100g finely chopped dried figs and 50g chopped walnuts for the caraway seeds and roasted cashews.

BAGELS

Bagels have become standard fare in coffee shops these days, filled with their traditional smoked salmon and cream cheese layers. And certainly a real bagel, with a firm shiny crust and a luscious chewy inside, is a super-tasty bread. So is it possible to replicate this magic at home? After many doughs and testings, I believe I have perfected not only a plain bagel, but also a new caraway and rye version that is delicious with cold meats, smoked fish or simply a schmeer of cream cheese. Try it. It's worth the effort.

Plain Bagels

These are better made over two days.

Makes 40

950g organic strong white bread flour
250g organic self-raising wholemeal flour
4 teaspoons dried yeast
1½ tablespoons fairtrade soft light brown sugar
2½ teaspoons salt
2 tablespoons light olive oil

For the cooking liquid
1 tablespoon fermented barley malt syrup or black molasses
1 tablespoon baking powder

1 organic free-range egg, beaten, to glaze
poppy, onion or sesame seeds, for the topping

In a medium bowl, combine 200g of the flour with 750ml lukewarm water, yeast and sugar and whisk until smooth. Make sure all the dried yeast has dissolved. Set aside in a warm place for about 10–15 minutes to ferment.

Combine the remaining flour with the salt in the bowl of your mixer. Pour the oil into the fermented yeast mixture and beat with a fork until smooth. With the mixer running, add the yeast mixture to the flour and mix to a soft, pliable dough. Turn out onto a floured work surface and knead for 5 minutes until smooth. Oil a large bowl and place the dough inside. Cover the top with oiled clingfilm or a cloth and set aside to rise in the fridge overnight.

The following day, divide the dough into 40 pieces and shape into balls. Roll each ball of dough into a sausage shape and form into bagels by overlapping the ends to form a ring. Allow a disproportionately large hole in the centre so there is space for the bagels to rise (otherwise the holes will close). Transfer the bagels to two or three baking sheets, lined with baking parchment and dusted with flour. Cover with a clean cloth and leave to prove in a warm place for 20 minutes until doubled in size.

Preheat the oven to 220°C/gas mark 7. Bring a large, wide pan of water to the boil. Add the malt syrup or black molasses and whisk in the baking powder. You will need to cook the bagels in batches. Carefully drop the bagels – three at a time – into the boiling water. Simmer for 2–3 minutes then quickly flip them over and cook them for another 2–3 minutes on the other side. Remove them with a slotted spoon and put them back on the baking parchment while you cook the rest. Once the bagels are cooked, glaze them with the beaten egg and sprinkle them with seeds. Bake in the preheated oven for 10–15 minutes until golden brown – and be proud!

Variation with Rye and Caraway

Substitute the flours for 950g organic strong white bread flour and 250g rye flour. For the topping, use 25g caraway seeds.

Bialys ℗

Bialys came from Bialystok, Russia, now in Central Poland. They made the journey to the United States in the early 1900s with Russian Jewish immigrants who began trading in the Lower East Side of New York.

They are an unusual bread, with a chewy and yeasty texture similar to a bagel but baked without the hole. The depression in the middle is usually filled with poppy seeds, garlic, chopped onion or flavoured breadcrumbs.

Makes 24

3 scant tablespoons dried yeast
4 teaspoons sugar
4 teaspoons salt
840g organic strong white bread flour
2 handfuls of coarse grain couscous or rye flour, for dusting

For the topping
125g minced onion or tahini (oriental sesame paste)
2 tablespoons poppy seeds
2 tablespoons sesame seeds
2 tablespoons vegetable oil
a pinch of salt

Pour 510ml warm water water into a large bowl, sprinkle in the yeast and whisk to dissolve the granules. Add the sugar, salt and flour and mix to a soft, pliable dough. Tip out onto a floured work surface and knead for 10–12 minutes. Shape the dough into a ball, place in a large, oiled bowl and turn it over so it is lightly coated in oil. Cover with oiled clingfilm and leave to rise somewhere warm for at least 30 minutes, or until doubled in size. Remove the clingfilm, punch out the air with your fist and return the dough to a warm place to rise for a further 30 minutes, or until doubled in size.

Meanwhile, prepare the topping by combining the minced onion or tahini with the seeds, oil and salt in a bowl.

Preheat the oven to 225°C/gas mark 7½ and dust two baking sheets with couscous or rye flour. Turn out the dough onto a floured work surface and cut into 4 pieces. Divide each piece into 6 balls and roll out to form circles 2cm thick. Arrange the dough on your prepared baking sheets and make an indentation in the centre of each, using a small shot glass to twist. Place a small teaspoon of topping in the centre. Cover with a clean cloth and place in a warm place to prove for about 20–30 minutes, or until doubled in size. Bake in the hot oven for 15–20 minutes.

Onion-layered Focaccia (P)

This delicious bread recipe pays its respects to the Italian Jewish communities. It is reworked from the traditional, omitting the large amounts of olive oil on the top, but with a mind to improving its keeping properties. Choose whether you add the thick seam of fried onions in the middle. Delicious with slices of wurst, cold meats or cheeses.

Makes 10 slices

1½ teaspoons dried yeast
500g organic strong white bread flour
2 large, sweet, white onions, finely sliced or chopped
2 tablespoons olive oil, plus extra for brushing
1½ teaspoons salt
50ml extra virgin olive oil

For the topping
coarse sea salt, to sprinkle
a handful of fresh rosemary sprigs
1 small red onion, cut in chunks

Place the dried yeast in a bowl with 2 tablespoons of the flour and whisk in 300ml warm water to a smooth paste. Set aside to ferment for about 15 minutes, or until bubbles appear on the surface.

Meanwhile, fry the white onions in 1 tablespoon of the olive oil until soft and just starting to colour. Set aside to cool.

Combine the remaining flour and salt in a large bowl (I use the bowl of my mixer with the dough hook attached). Add the extra virgin olive oil to the yeast mixture and beat with a fork until smooth. Pour the mixture into the bowl with the flour and combine to a soft, pliable dough. Tip out onto a floured work surface and knead for a few minutes until smooth. The dough will seem very soft, but it is the extra liquid in this mixture that makes the bread so moist. Place the dough in an oiled bowl, cover with oiled clingfilm or a clean cloth and set aside to rise in a warm place for about 30 minutes until doubled in size.

Preheat the oven to 200°C/gas mark 6 and smear a large roasting tray (32 x 25 x 7cm) with olive oil. Tip out the dough onto a floured work surface and cut into 2 pieces. Roll out one piece of dough to fit your prepared roasting tray and scatter with the cooled, cooked onions. Roll out the remaining piece of dough and lay it carefully over the top. Using your fingers, make little dimples all over the surface of the bread and then brush lightly with the remaining tablespoon olive oil. Sprinkle with the sea salt, spear with tiny little rosemary sprigs and scatter over the raw onion. Place the tray in a warm place (do not cover it this time) and leave to prove for about 30 minutes until nicely puffed up.

Bake in the hot oven for about 25 minutes or until gloriously fragrant and golden. Serve straight away or reheat the following day in the microwave. This bread freezes beautifully.

Variation
Omit the layer of cooked onions and roll out the dough to make two thinner breads. As an alternative to red onion on top, try a scattering of stoned olives.

CHALLAH (THE SABBATH BREAD)

'Blessed art thou oh Lord our G-d, King of the Universe, who has sanctified us by thy commandments, and commanded us to set aside Challah from the dough.'

This small prayer is said in the home when a portion of challah dough is removed and burnt to remember the Temple sacrifice before baking. Challah's origins reach back to the time when the Jews were in the desert and were given an extra portion of manna for the Sabbath so they would not have to work picking it up that day. The Bible also mentions that Isaac's wife Rivka made challah every Friday, and so a tradition evolved to make the bread as perfect and beautiful as possible – celebrating the Sabbath or holidays, with white flour, in contrast to the rough, brown Ashkenazi bread that the poor Jews ate during the week.

On the Friday night Kiddush or before a festival, wine is used saying a blessing followed by the challah – dipped either in salt or, on the New Year, in honey to signify a good sweet year.

Please try this recipe enriched with soya milk and saffron to taste the most melting silken dough with a rich crisp crust.

Super-rich Challah (P)

Makes 4 large loaves or 40 bulkies (rolls from Challah dough)

385ml warm soya milk
2 generous pinches ground saffron (about ⅛ teaspoon)
2 tablespoons dried yeast
1 tablespoon fairtrade soft brown sugar
1 tablespoon honey
1 tablespoon golden syrup
1kg organic strong white bread flour – the best you can buy
3 teaspoons salt
5 organic free-range eggs, plus 2 egg yolks for the mixture
    and 1 egg yolk for glazing
115g light olive oil, plus extra for greasing
poppy seeds, sesame seeds or even hundreds and thousands, to decorate

(If you can't find ground saffron, just add 4 generous pinches of saffron strands to 40ml of hot water. When this water is bright yellow/orange (about 10 minutes), strain and add this liquid to the remaining water, ensuring the total quantity is 240ml.)

In a small bowl, combine 240ml warm water with the warm milk, saffron, yeast, sugar, honey, golden syrup and about 100g of the flour. Whisk until smooth and no yeast lumps remain. Set aside in a warm place to ferment for about 20 minutes until the mixture is bubbling (I put the bowl on the hob above my lit oven).

In a large mixing bowl, combine the remaining flour with the salt (I use my mixer with the dough hook attached). Beat all of the eggs into the bowl with the yeast mixture, pour in the oil and beat with a fork until smooth. Pour the wet ingredients into the mixing bowl with the flour and mix to a soft, pliable dough. You may need to add a little more oil or flour, depending on the dryness of the mixture. Place the dough in a large, clean, oiled bowl, cover with a cloth or oiled clingfilm and leave to rise in a warm place for 40–60 minutes or until doubled in size. Alternatively, leave to rise overnight in the fridge, which definitely improves the flavour.

Preheat the oven to 200°C/gas mark 6 and line two baking sheets with baking parchment. Tip out the risen dough onto a floured work surface and knock out the air with your fists. Either form into two large round twists for the New Year, or shape into plaits or individual rolls called bulkies. Place on your prepared baking trays, cover with a clean cloth or oiled clingfilm and set aside to prove in a warm place for 30–40 minutes until doubled in size. Make an egg wash by beating together the remaining egg with a little oil and glaze the challah all over. Sprinkle with seeds and bake in the hot oven for about 30–35 minutes until golden. Bulkies will take about 20 minutes. You will know when they are cooked because they will sound hollow when you tap them on the base.

Variation
For Rosh Hashanah and Purim, when a sweet challah may be needed, add 100g raisins soaked in about 2 tablespoons orange juice (or Kiddush wine for the ultimate flavour). Mix it at the end, after the egg and yeast mixture, to retain their shape.

Delicious Challah

Low Cholesterol, Half the Calories, but High on Flavour

I almost feel there should be a fanfare of trumpets to announce the birth of this challah, devised to feed my wonderful husband who suffers from high cholesterol. After six attempts, I added ground saffron, which gave the finished loaf a wonderful flavour and a lovely golden eggy colour (even though the recipe doesn't contain any eggs). Substituting olive oil for butter or margarine results in an incredibly moist loaf. I tend to make a large quantity as the bread freezes really well.

Makes 2 large loaves

925g strong organic bread flour
2 large pinches of ground saffron (about ⅛ teaspoon)
1 tablespoon dried yeast
1½ teaspoons sugar
3½ teaspoons salt
100ml light olive oil
1 organic free-range egg, beaten, to glaze
poppy or sesame seeds, for the topping

In a small bowl, combine 100g of the flour with 600ml warm water and saffron. (If you can't find ground saffron, simply soak a generous pinch of saffron strands in the warm water beforehand and strain the liquid into the bowl.) Add the dried yeast and sugar and whisk until smooth. Make sure all the dried yeast has dissolved. Set aside in a warm place for about 20 minutes to ferment.

Combine the remaining flour with the salt in the bowl of your mixer. Pour the olive oil into the fermented yeast mixture and beat with a fork until smooth. With the mixer running, add the yeast mixture to the flour. Then, with your hands, knead the mix in the bowl into a soft, pliable dough. You may need to add a little extra water or flour if necessary – the wetter the dough, the lighter the challah.

Place the dough in an oiled bowl, cover with a cloth or clingfilm and leave to rise in a warm place for about 1 hour until doubled in size. Alternatively, set aside to rise in the fridge overnight.

Preheat the oven to 220°C/gas mark 7 and line two baking sheets with baking parchment. Tip out the dough onto a floured work surface and divide into four pieces. Shape into loaves and transfer them to the prepared baking sheets. Cover with a cloth or oiled clingfilm and leave to prove in a warm place for 30 minutes until doubled in size. Glaze with the beaten egg and sprinkle with seeds. Bake in the oven for about 30 minutes until golden brown. You will know when the bread is cooked because it will sound hollow when you tap it on the base. Enjoy.

BUCKWHEAT BLINI

Buckwheat, part of Jewish Eastern-European food heritage, is a living anomaly. For it bears no relation to wheat and, although considered a grain, is actually a grass seed called an achene. Wherever it was planted, it became part of the food culture of that nation – often developing legendary status. Russians, Ukrainians and Poles roasted the 'groats' to form the dough for filled knishes or blintzes, or mixed it with lokshen bows to make kasha varnishkes (kasha oats cooked to a soft mix with bow pasta). Ground into flour, the mid-Western pioneers stored it in covered wagons for simple nutritious pancakes. The French created crêpes, while the Russians made blinis – soft mouth-watering delicacies – the food of legend.

Healthy Yeasted Blini

A luscious homemade blini was the challenge! These blinis are choc-full of flavour, delicious served with fried mushrooms or traditional smoked salmon and horseradish topping. Well worth the effort.

Makes 20 blini

½ teaspoon sugar
½ teaspoon dried yeast
Either 70g buckwheat flour plus 80g strong wholemeal flour
   or 150g buckwheat flour
250ml lukewarm soya milk
½ teaspoon salt
1 scant tablespoon olive oil, plus extra for frying
1 organic free-range egg

In a large mixing bowl, whisk together the sugar, yeast, 2 tablespoons of the flour and the warm milk. Set aside to ferment in a warm place for about 15 minutes until bubbles appear on the surface.

Beat in the remaining flour, salt and olive oil. Separate the egg and beat the yolk into the mixture. Cover the bowl with clingfilm and set aside to rise in a warm place for about 15 minutes until the mixture bubbles. Meanwhile, whisk the egg white until soft peaks form. Fold the beaten egg white into the blini mixture.

Heat a little oil in a non-stick frying pan until medium hot – not smoking. Drop dainty ladlefuls of the blini mixture into the pan. Wait for bubbles to appear on the surface and then flip them over and cook on the other side. Keep warm while you cook the rest. Serve with the topping of your choice and enjoy.

CROISSANTS

The croissant, part of the French Jewish tradition, has always been known as a super high-fat bread. However, here we have given it a low-cholesterol makeover in answer to the pleas of our *Jewish Chronicle* readers.

A Healthier Jewish Croissant

 or Ⓜ

Makes 32 small croissants

195ml skimmed or soya milk
10g teaspoons dried yeast
590g plain flour
1 tablespoons honey
300g plain or wholemeal flour
3 teaspoons salt
120g cholesterol-lowering spread or dairy-free margarine, at room temperature
4 tablespoons fairtrade soft brown sugar
3 organic free-range eggs
olive oil, for brushing
100g poppy seeds

Warm the milk and 100ml water to body temperature and then whisk in the yeast with 2 tablespoons plain flour. Stir in the honey and set aside in a warm place to ferment for about 15 minutes, or until the surface is bubbling and frothy.

Meanwhile, combine the remaining flours with the salt in a large mixing bowl. Add the cholesterol-lowering spread and rub in with your fingertips to form a breadcrumb-like mixture. Stir in the sugar.

Break the eggs into the yeast mixture and beat well with a fork to combine. Pour the yeast mixture into the mixing bowl with the flour and mix to a soft dough. Turn out onto a floured surface and knead for 5–10 minutes until smooth. Place the dough in an oiled bowl, cover with oiled clingfilm or a clean cloth and set aside to rise in the fridge overnight until doubled in size.

Preheat the oven to 200°C/gas mark 6 and line two or three baking sheets with baking parchment. Tip the dough out onto a floured work surface and divide it into 4 pieces. Cut each piece into 4 to give 16 pieces in total. Roll out each piece to form a square, 10 x 10 cm, and then cut diagonally to give equal triangles. Roll out each triangle as thinly as possible and brush lightly with olive oil. Sprinkle with poppy seeds and then roll up the triangles of pastry to form Swiss-roll shapes, starting with the widest side first. Twist to form crescents, brush with a little more oil and then transfer to your prepared baking sheets. Set aside in a warm place to prove for 30–40 minutes until doubled in size.

When puffy, glaze with beaten egg and bake in the hot oven for 15 minutes until golden and fragrant.

Variation
Use sesame or onion seeds in place of the poppy seeds. For an indulgent filling, spread the triangles of pastry with low-fat cheese before rolling them up.

10: Passover

'And this day shall be unto you for a memorial and ye shall keep it a feast to the Lord, throughout your generations ye shall keep it as a feast by an ordinance forever.'

EXODUS 12:14

There is an air of excitement before the Passover service. A white cloth laid with silver and the best china affirms that slavery is past. Children wait to find the Afikoman, a broken piece of matzo hidden by the celebrant and exchanged later for a present.

In front of the celebrant is a beautiful plate laid with three perfect matzot not touching each other and wrapped in a cloth. Next to the matzot is a Seder plate – an elaborate platter of metal or china, laid with symbolic foods. After the first prayers, the special foods are eaten: matzo, unleavened Passover bread, spread with bitter horseradish (maror) to signify the tears cried by Jewish slaves. Then a spiced apple, nut and wine mixture formed into a mortar-type paste (haroseth), representing the bricks that the slaves formed in the hot Egyptian sun. The meal begins with hard-boiled eggs (baytzah), iconic symbols of life and rebirth, eaten with salt water to symbolise the tears of slavery. All these are relished with reverential blessings, while the roasted egg, commemorating the Passover sacrifice, nestles next to the Pascal lamb bone (zeroa) on the Seder plate, referring to the tenth plague when the Egyptian first born were killed and G-d 'passed over' the Jewish homes with blood on their doorposts. Some sources say that these small offerings were the very first biblical starters.

Passover, or Pesach, is a backbreaking time in a Jewish household – it's necessary to clean every surface that has seen leavened bread – and there are numerous special foods to prepare. In order to ease the load, here are traditional and new recipes, some to freeze in advance, to help with the problems of Passover preparation and hopefully provide exciting inspiration.

Foragers' Pie

Serves 4–6

Although the Bible orders us to feast, the cooks in the house need food that is easy to prepare, especially on Passover Eve. Mushrooms have always been a focus of Jewish food and this foragers' pie would be perfect for a pre-Seder meal, when eating matzo and other flours is forbidden and the Passover meal is still hours away. This dish will also suit vegetarians as a main course for Passover.

700g floury potatoes, such as Desirée, peeled and cut into large chunks
about 850ml vegetable stock (enough to cover the potatoes)
freshly ground salt and black pepper
6 medium or 4 large onions (about 800g), finely sliced
1 tablespoon olive oil
800g fresh mushrooms, roughly chopped
4 large organic free-range eggs
25g fresh flat-leaf parsley, finely chopped

Preheat the oven to 180°C/gas mark 4. Place the potatoes in a large pan, pour over the vegetable stock to cover and boil until tender. Drain, keeping back 3 tablespoons of stock, and return to the pan. Mash thoroughly with the stock, season well and set aside to cool slightly.

Meanwhile, gently fry the onions in the oil until soft but not coloured. Add the mushrooms and cook until all the liquid has evaporated. Stir in the parsley and season well. Spoon the mixture into the base of a deep 2-litre oven-to-table dish.

Separate the eggs and add the yolks to the potato mixture, beating in well. Whisk the egg whites until stiff and fold into the potato mixture. Pile the potatoes on top of the mushrooms and bake in the oven for 1 hour until golden brown on top. Serve with a large watercress, orange and walnut salad.

Variations
For a bit of heat, add 1 finely chopped chilli to the mushroom mixture. For a more substantial vegetarian main course, add a layer of grilled or roasted peppers and aubergines. You can also add 150–200g grated cheese to the potato mixture (or simply grate it over the top), which will make the dish *milchig*.

Carrot and Almond Bake

This delicious soufflé-like carrot bake was invented for vegetarians. But it seems the carnivores adore its sweet fluffy texture too.

Serves 10

1kg carrots, peeled and roughly chopped
1 Passover vegetable stock cube
3 large onions, peeled and roughly chopped
1 tablespoon olive oil
25g fresh parsley or coriander, finely chopped
freshly ground salt and black pepper
200g ground almonds
6 organic free-range eggs
200g flaked almonds

Preheat the oven to 180°C/gas mark 4 and grease two 2-litre oven-to-table dishes. Place the carrots in a pan, pour over enough water to barely cover, crumble in the stock cube and cook until tender.

Meanwhile, in a separate pan, gently fry the onions in the oil until soft and just starting to colour. Drain the carrots and blitz to a smooth purée with the onions and herbs. Scoop out into a bowl and stir in the ground almonds and some salt and pepper.

Separate the eggs and add the yolks to the carrot and almond mixture. Whisk the whites until stiff peaks form and carefully fold in. Spoon the mixture into your prepared dishes and scatter over the flaked almonds. Bake for 1 hour.

Huevos Haminados

This Sephardic dish was created by clever balabosters for Pesach. After cooking, the creamy brown eggs can be enjoyed as a snack, sliced over a salad, or added to a main course for extra protein.

Serves 8

plenty of onion skins (ideally about 20)
8 organic free-range eggs
2 tablespoons olive oil
1 tablespoon Turkish coffee
2 teaspoons salt
1½ teaspoons black pepper

Place half of the onion skins in the base of a heavy-based pan and carefully nestle the eggs on top. Put in the rest of the ingredients, cover with the remaining onion skins and pour over enough water to cover.

Bring to the boil and simmer, covered, for at least 8 hours (preferably overnight). Remove the eggs with a slotted spoon and place in a bowl of iced water. Serve peeled and enjoy either hot or cold.

Herby Gnocchi in Mushroom Sauce

It's that 'what to do for lunch' predicament that prompted this recipe. And how exciting to borrow ideas from another culture to create a Passover dish.

Serves 4–6

For the gnocchi
1kg large floury potatoes, such as Desirée
1 tablespoon oil, plus extra for brushing
1 organic free-range egg
15g fresh basil
15g fresh flat-leaf parsley
freshly ground salt and black pepper
4 tablespoons potato flour, plus extra for dusting

For the mushroom sauce
3 large sweet Spanish onions, finely sliced
1 tablespoon olive oil
1 garlic clove, peeled and crushed (optional)
450g mixed mushrooms, cleaned and roughly chopped
1 x 300g tub of Passover cream cheese
1 red chilli, finely chopped (optional)
freshly ground salt and black pepper
a handful of fresh parsley or basil, finely chopped, to garnish

Preheat the oven to 200°C/gas mark 6. Brush the potatoes with oil, prick them with a skewer and place on a roasting tin. Bake in the oven for 40 minutes to 1 hour until tender and golden.

Meanwhile, make the mushroom sauce. In a large frying pan, gently fry the onion in the olive oil until soft and translucent. Add the crushed garlic and mushrooms and cook until they release their juices. Fold in the cream cheese and chilli (if using), plus some salt and pepper and set aside.

Cut the potatoes in half and scrape out the insides into a bowl. (Return the skins to the oven to crisp up for a delicious high-fibre nosh!) Pass the flesh through a ricer or sieve back into the bowl. It should still be relatively warm.

Place the egg, oil, herbs and seasoning in a food-processor and blitz to a smooth purée. Scrape into the bowl with the potato, sift in the potato flour and mix to a soft dough. Dust your work surface with potato flour and roll out the dough into long sausages, 3cm in diameter. (If necessary, you may need to add a little more potato flour depending on the moisture of your potatoes.) Cut into 3cm lengths and decorate with grooves using the tines of a fork.

To cook the gnocchi, bring a large pan of salted water to the boil. Drop in the gnocchi and wait for them to rise to the surface – about 3–5 minutes. Drain through a colander and serve with the sauce. Garnish with parsley or basil.

Variation
Use tomato sauce in place of the mushroom sauce (see page 134).

Spinach and Cheesy Leek Roulade (M)

This isn't usually made for Passover, but it makes a delicious lunch.

Serves 6–8

3 large leeks (about 380g), sliced into fine rings and washed really well
1 tablespoon olive oil
1kg spinach, washed really well
25g fresh flat-leaf parsley or chives
freshly ground salt and black pepper
8 organic free-range eggs
70g potato flour
70g fine matzo meal
1 medium-hot chilli (seeds discarded), finely chopped (optional)
300ml Passover soft cheese

Preheat the oven to 190°C/gas mark 5 and line a Swiss-roll tin with baking parchment. In a large pan, gently fry the leeks in the oil for 5 minutes until tender. Remove and set aside in a small bowl.

Add the washed spinach to the pan and cook for a few minutes, turning, until it wilts. Drain well and chop or process along with the herbs. Place in a large mixing bowl and season with salt and pepper. Separate the eggs and add the yolks to the spinach, beating in well. Sift in the potato flour and matzo meal and fold in carefully.

In a separate bowl, whisk the egg whites until stiff and fold into the spinach mixture. Spoon into your prepared tin, level the top with a palette knife and bake for 10–15 minutes until firm to the touch.

To make the filling, add the chilli to the cooked leeks and beat in the cheese. Spread a clean piece of baking parchment on your work surface. Remove the roulade from the oven and place it upside down on the parchment paper. Carefully peel off the paper from the base and spread the leek and cheese filling evenly over the roulade. Roll up the roulade, Swiss roll-style, and transfer to a decorative dish. Serve warm or cold, as you prefer.

Cauliflower Pancakes (Chremslach) Ⓜ

These pancakes are very delicate, so they need to be handled carefully. Despite being fried, they have a high vegetable content that makes them relatively healthy.
Makes 13–14 generous pancakes (Serves 4 for a light lunch)

500g cauliflower florets – frozen is fine
1 Passover vegetable stock cube
2 small onions (about 160g), finely chopped
1 tablespoon olive oil, plus extra for shallow-frying
½–1 red chilli, seeds removed (optional)
150g fine matzo meal
1–2 teaspoons salt
3 organic free-range eggs
375ml milk

Place the cauliflower in a pan, cover with water and crumble in the stock cube. Bring to the boil and cook until tender. Drain very well on absorbent kitchen paper.

Meanwhile, in a large frying pan, gently fry the onion in the oil until soft but not coloured. Tip the onion into a food-processor, add the cauliflower and chilli (if using) and blitz to a smooth purée. Scoop out into a large mixing bowl.

Place the matzo meal and salt into a separate bowl, break in the eggs, pour in the milk and whisk thoroughly to form a smooth batter. Pour into the cauliflower mixture, and beat until smooth. Set aside for about 10 minutes to allow the matzo meal to swell.

To cook the pancakes, heat 1 tablespoon oil in a large frying pan over a medium-high heat. Spoon the batter into the pan, about a tablespoon at a time, and cook for 2–3 minutes on each side until golden brown. Serve with chraine and a generous green salad livened up with orange and grapefruit segments and chopped pecan nuts.

Nutty Passover Rolls

My mother made these choux pastry-style rolls as a tempting change from matzos.
Makes 40 small rolls

450g fine matzo meal
2 teaspoons salt
4 teaspoons caster sugar
100g toasted nibbed almonds or chopped walnuts
240ml light olive oil
8 organic free-range eggs

Preheat the oven to 190°C/gas mark 5 and line two baking sheets with baking parchment. Sift the matzo meal into a mixing bowl and add the salt and sugar. Toast the almonds or walnuts in a dry frying pan until they start to colour, tip onto a plate and set aside to cool.

In a heavy-based pan, heat 475ml water with the oil until it comes to a rolling boil. Quickly tip in the matzo meal and beat hard over the heat until the mixture starts to come away from the sides of the pan. Remove from the heat and set aside to cool slightly. Beat the eggs in a large jug and slowly add them to the pan, beating really well between each addition. Keep beating until the mixture is glossy and smooth. Fold in the toasted nuts and set aside to cool.

Shape the mixture into 40 golfball-sized balls and arrange on the prepared baking sheets, spacing them out to allow room for them to spread. Bake in the oven for 25 minutes until lusciously golden.

EASY PASSOVER CAKES

Passover, with its flour ban, creates difficulties for the most adept of bakers and many people crave inspiration. Here are a series of traditional cakes, along with some new, more tempting ideas.

Passover Sponge

 or (M)

Begin with a basic (almost Victoria) sponge and make it your own with a whole host of different flavours to choose from.

Serves 8

For the basic cake:
125g Passover margarine or butter
125g caster sugar
1 tablespoon vanilla sugar
4 organic free-range eggs
95g cake meal
95g potato flour
1½ teaspoons Passover baking powder
a pinch of salt
3 tablespoons milk or water
6–8 tablespoons jam of your choice
caster sugar, for dusting

Preheat the oven to 180°C/gas mark 4 and line an 18cm round cake tin with baking parchment.

In a mixing bowl, cream the margarine or butter with the sugars until light and fluffy. Separate the eggs and beat in the yolks only. Sift in the cake meal, potato flour and baking powder, and fold in carefully. In a separate bowl, whisk the egg whites with a pinch of salt until soft peaks form. Add a spoonful of the egg white to the cake batter and mix in thoroughly. Now fold in the rest of the eggs whites, taking care not to knock out any air. Spoon the mixture into your prepared tin and bake for 35–40 minutes until risen and golden.

After the cake has cooled, slice in half horizontally and spread the bottom half with jam. Replace the top half and sprinkle caster sugar over the top.

Variations

Coffee and walnut cake (pictured): Add 2 tablespoons instant coffee powder dissolved in 1 tablespoon hot water and 100g chopped walnuts. Fold in before you add the egg whites. For coffee icing combine 200g sieved icing sugar with 1½–2 tablespoons strong black coffee. Beat well and pour over the cake. Decorate with extra walnuts.

Lemon/orange and vanilla cake: Add the grated zest of 1 lemon or orange and 1 tablespoon vanilla sugar. Cream with the margarine and sugar.

Fruit cake: Soak 150g mixed dried fruit in the juice of 1 orange or lemon until plump. Add with the egg yolks.

Carrot cake: Add 175g grated carrot, the zest of 1 orange, and the juice of ½ lemon. Add with the egg yolks.

Almond cake: Add 2 drops of almond extract. Cream with the margarine and sugar. Sprinkle the top with 100g flaked almonds before baking.

Lemon drizzle cake: Add the grated zest of 1 lemon. Cream with the margarine and sugar. Combine 50ml lemon juice with 125ml granulated sugar and pour over the hot cake when it comes out of the oven.

Chocolate cake: Melt 175ml Passover chocolate and fold in before adding the egg whites.

Cinnamon apple cake: Spread the cake mixture into a lined Swiss-roll-style tin. Layer over 450g peeled and sliced apples. Sprinkle with 100g caster sugar and dust with 1 heaped teaspoon ground cinnamon. Bake and then cut into squares. Serve with Kosher Dairy Substitute Whip.

Rich Chocolate and Matzo Cake

This ultra-rich cake has been enjoyed in my family for generations. Its moist layers are a perfect marriage with good coffee. Use the leftover egg whites for Meringue Pillows (see page 224), Macaroons (page 222) or pavlova.

Serves 12–16 (small portions)

120g Passover margarine
140g fairtrade soft light brown or golden caster sugar
4 tablespoons cocoa powder
2 heaped tablespoons instant coffee
10 organic, free-range egg yolks
7 large matzos
3–4 teaspoons strong black coffee (or red wine)
70g whole toasted almonds, to decorate

Place the margarine, sugar, cocoa powder and coffee powder in a large, heavy-based saucepan and stir over a low heat until the margarine has melted. Remove from the heat and set aside to cool slightly.

Add the egg yolks, beating well to give a glossy, thick chocolate sauce. (If the sauce fails to thicken, pour the mixture into a glass bowl and set over a pan of barely simmering water. Stir gently until the mixture thickens.)

To assemble the cake, quickly dip a matzo into the coffee (or wine) to moisten it and arrange on a decorative plate. Spoon over a layer of the chocolate sauce and top with another coffee (or wine) flavoured matzo. Layer up the remaining matzos and chocolate sauce and sprinkle with toasted almonds. Set aside to cool. To serve, cut into small squares with a sharp knife and enjoy with a cup of coffee.

Wonderful Passover Pastry (P)

This amended pastry recipe pays homage to the late Evelyn Rose. This pastry will make a generous apple tart to serve 10, easy pastry biscuits rolled in a strudel shape with dried fruit and jam, or one portion of jam tarts. It freezes perfectly and so can be prepared in advance.

Makes 1.1kg

300g Passover margarine
175g fairtrade soft light brown sugar
10g vanilla sugar
zest of 1 lemon
zest of 1 orange
225g cake meal
225g potato flour
225g ground almonds or ground hazelnuts
3 organic free-range eggs
juice of ½ lemon

In a large mixing bowl, cream the margarine with the sugars and zests until light and fluffy. In a separate bowl, sift the cake meal and potato flour and stir in the ground almonds. Combine the dry ingredients with the margarine mixture and beaten eggs, adding enough lemon juice to mix to a soft dough. Wrap in clingfilm and chill in the fridge for 30 minutes before use. Use as required.

Blueprint for the Perfect Plava (P)

At last, you can make the Plava of your dreams! This one is light as a feather, moist and freezes well. To make it extra special, split and layer with lemon curd (see page 233) and drizzle with a sharp lemon icing. To make the icing, combine 200g sieved icing sugar with the juice of 1 lemon.

Serves 10–12

12 organic free-range eggs
300g caster sugar
15g vanilla sugar
grated zest and juice of 1 lemon
juice of ½ orange
75g cake meal
75g potato flour
70g ground almonds
icing sugar, to dust

Preheat the oven to 170°C/gas mark 3 and grease and flour a square or round 27cm springform cake tin. Separate the eggs and place the yolks in a large mixing bowl. Add the caster sugar, vanilla sugar and lemon zest and beat together until thick and creamy. In a separate bowl, whisk the egg whites until stiff peaks form. In a separate bowl, sift the cake meal with the potato flour (twice if possible) and stir in the ground almonds. Fold the dry ingredients into the egg yolk mixture, along with the orange and lemon juice, and then carefully fold in the egg whites.

Pour into your prepared cake tin and bake for 1¼ hours. When cool, dust with icing sugar.

Chocolate, Raspberry and Cream Torte (P)

A chocoholic's dream, this ultra-moist cake looks more complicated than it is.

Serves 10

175g Passover dark chocolate (70 per cent cocoa solids)
6 organic free-range eggs
175g Passover soft dark or light brown sugar (if unavailable use caster sugar)
2 tablespoons Passover cocoa powder, sifted
1 x 425ml tub Kosher Dairy Substitute Whip
2 tablespoons kirsch, brandy or Kiddush wine (optional)
2 punnets (about 300g) of fresh raspberries or blueberries
icing sugar and a few squares of Passover dark chocolate, to decorate

Preheat the oven to 180°C/gas mark 4 and grease and flour a round springform cake tin, 21cm in diameter.

Break the chocolate into squares and place in a glass bowl over a pan of gently simmering water, ensuring the bowl is not in contact with the water. Carefully stir the chocolate until it has melted. Leave to cool.

Separate the eggs and place the yolks in a large mixing bowl. Using electric beaters, if possible, whisk the egg yolks with the sugar until the mixture is really thick and creamy. Beat in 2 tablespoons cocoa powder.

In a separate bowl, whisk the egg whites until stiff peaks form. Add 1 tablespoon to the egg yolk mixture and stir in to loosen the mixture, and then carefully fold in the rest. Finally fold in the melted chocolate. Pour into the prepared tin and bake for about 20 minutes until firm to the touch. Remove from the oven and leave to cool in the tin before turning out onto a decorative plate.

To decorate, beat the Dairy Substitute Whip with the alcohol (if using). Wash the fruit, dry on kitchen paper and fold half into the Whip. Pile on top of the cake and decorate with the remaining fruit. To finish, dust with icing sugar and grate over a little chocolate. Chill in the fridge until needed.

Date and Orange Chocolate Brownies

 or

Sometimes Passover cakes can be dry, but this combination of soaked dried dates and gooey chocolate will keep both adults and children happy.

Serves 6–8

200g chopped dried dates
30ml brandy or orange juice
275g Passover dark chocolate (70 per cent cocoa solids)
275g Passover margarine or butter
100g cake meal
75g potato flour
1 teaspoon Passover baking powder
4 large organic free-range eggs
1 teaspoon vanilla extract
grated zest of 1 orange
325g fairtrade soft dark brown sugar or caster sugar
150g Passover chocolate chips

Preheat the oven to 180°C/gas mark 4 and line a 21cm square tin with baking parchment.

Place the dates in a saucepan with the brandy or orange juice and heat gently until the dates are softened (10–15 minutes), stirring occasionally. Remove from the heat and set aside to plump up.

Break the chocolate into squares and place in a glass bowl with the margarine. Set over a pan of gently simmering water, making sure the base of the bowl doesn't come into contact with the water, and stir gently until the chocolate melts. Set aside to cool.

In a separate bowl, sift the cake meal with the potato flour and baking powder. In a large mixing bowl, whisk the eggs with the vanilla essence, sugar and orange zest until light and creamy. Stir in the melted chocolate, dates and chocolate chips, fold in the flours and spoon into the prepared cake tin. Bake in the oven for 40–50 minutes until firm on top, but still slightly gooey in the centre.

Pesach Double Chocolate Orange Cookies

Perfect to make with children.

Makes 24

110g cake meal
20g cocoa powder
40g ground almonds, ground hazelnuts or ground mixed nuts
120g soft Passover margarine
170g fairtrade soft light brown sugar (or caster sugar)
grated zest of 1 large orange
2 organic free-range eggs
100g Passover dark chocolate (70 per cent cocoa solids), finely chopped

Preheat the oven to 170°C/gas mark 3 and line two baking sheets with baking parchment.

In a large bowl, sift the cake meal with the cocoa powder and stir in the ground nuts. In a mixing bowl, beat the margarine and sugar with the orange zest until light and fluffy. Add the eggs a little at a time, beating well between each addition. Fold in the dry ingredients, along with 70g of the chopped chocolate.

Drop teaspoons of the mixture onto your prepared baking sheets, allowing space in between for them to spread. Sprinkle over the remaining chocolate, pressing it down slightly with your fingers. Bake in the oven for 15–20 minutes until the cookies have a firm crust – they will firm up even more as they cool.

Toffee'd Almonds ⓟ

A crunchy alternative to chocolate and my grandchildren's favourite part of Passover preparations.

Makes 500g

300g flaked almonds
200g white granulated sugar
vegetable oil, for greasing

Preheat the oven to 170°C/gas mark 3 and grease a baking sheet with a little oil.

Scatter the almonds over a roasting tin and toast in the oven for 5–10 minutes until lightly golden – keep an eye on them and shake the tin occasionally because they can burn easily.

Place the sugar in a heavy-based pan with 225ml water and swirl over a low heat until the sugar dissolves. Bring to the boil and bubble vigorously until a golden caramel colour is reached. Remove from the heat very carefully and quickly tip in the toasted almonds. Pour the mixture onto your greased tin and spread out slightly with a palette knife. Set aside to cool and then break into pieces or shards. Store in a well-sealed container. Serve as a delicious Passover sweet.

Variation
Melt 200g dark Passover chocolate in a bowl above a pan of boiling water. Drizzle the chocolate over the shards of brittle.

Wafer Biscuits

These crisp, lemony wafer biscuits are something to enjoy with a drink.

Makes 30–35

65g Passover margarine
1 organic free-range egg
65g caster sugar
grated zest of 1 lemon
25g fine matzo meal
25g potato flour

Preheat the oven to 220°C/gas mark 7 and line two baking sheets with baking parchment.

Place the margarine in a small saucepan and melt over a low heat. Set aside to cool slightly.

In a large mixing bowl, whisk the egg with the sugar. Pour in the melted margarine, add the lemon zest and beat together until light and creamy. Sift the matzo meal and potato flour together and add to the mixture. Set aside for about 20 minutes to allow the matzo meal to swell.

Drop teaspoons of the mixture onto your baking sheets, allowing plenty of space in between for them to spread. Bake in the oven for about 5 minutes until golden and set. Remove from the parchment with a palette knife and transfer to a wire rack to cool.

Coconut Pyramids

When I was young, my late mother had a little plastic gadget – a pyramid with a stopper through the centre – to shape these like miniature sandcastles. The plastic gadget has gone but the taste remains delectable.

Makes about 20

2 organic free-range eggs
120g caster sugar
225g desiccated coconut

Preheat the oven to 180°C/gas mark 4 and line two baking sheets with baking parchment.

In a large mixing bowl, beat the eggs with the sugar until light and creamy. Stir in the desiccated coconut and mix to a stiff paste. Using wet hands, shape the mixture into pyramids and arrange on the baking sheet. Bake in the oven for 15–20 minutes until pale golden brown.

Cinnamon Macaroons

The perfumed fragrance of cinnamon and almond signifies another Passover. And cinnamon balls have to be the ultimate Ashkenazi Passover cookie. But try these crisp, elegant macaroons and compare.

Makes 36

3 organic free-range egg whites
225g caster sugar
175g ground almonds
1 tablespoon ground cinnamon

Preheat the oven to 170°C/gas mark 3 and line two baking sheets with baking parchment.

Beat the egg whites and sugar until stiff peaks form. Fold in the ground almonds and cinnamon. Using wet hands, roll the mixture into walnut-sized balls. Arrange on your prepared baking sheets, allowing plenty of space in between for them to spread. Bake in the oven for 25–30 minutes until crisp and toasted.

Delicious Fruit Nuggets ⓟ

These Passover nuggets were devised following *Jewish Chronicle* readers' requests for something easy and relatively healthy.

Makes about 20

150g dried peaches or apricots, chopped
150g sultanas
150g stoned dates, chopped
grated zest and juice of ½ lemon
grated zest and juice of ½ orange
200g ground almonds
Passover chocolate vermicelli, cocoa powder or desiccated coconut, to decorate

Place the fruit in a saucepan, squeeze over the orange and lemon juice and simmer for about 10 minutes until soft. Pour into a food-processor and blitz until smooth. (If you don't have a food-processor, simply chop the fruit very finely.)

Scrape the mixture into a bowl and fold in the grated zest and ground almonds. Shape into walnut-sized balls and roll in chocolate vermicelli, cocoa or desiccated coconut. Set aside in the fridge to firm up.

Variation
For spicy nutty nuggets, substitute 150g chopped walnuts for the peaches or apricots. Flavour with 1 teaspoon ground cinnamon and ¼ teaspoon ground ginger. For an adult flavour, soak the dried fruit in brandy instead of fruit juice and dip the nuggets in melted chocolate.

Meringue Pillows (P)

Makes 40

This meringue recipe breaks all the rules, but produces a crisp, crunchy, chewy toffee-like meringue.

Makes 40

5 organic free-range egg whites (10 fl oz in total)
300g icing sugar, sifted
15g vanilla sugar

Preheat the oven to 130°C/gas mark 1 and line two baking sheets with baking parchment. Place the egg whites in a bowl and whisk until soft peaks form (if possible, use an electric mixer). Slowly add the sugar, whisking all the time until the mixture is silky and thick. Place half of the meringue mixture in a separate bowl and flavour with coconut or almonds (see below), if you wish.

To cook, place teaspoons of the mixture onto the baking sheets and bake in the oven for approximately 1 hour.

Variations

For Coconut Clouds: Add 200g desiccated coconut, toasted first in a low oven at 150°C/gas mark 2 until golden. Fold into the meringue mixture.

For Almond Drops: Add 200g ground almonds, 2 tablespoons cake meal and a few drops almond extract. Fold into the meringue mixture, pipe or drop onto your baking sheets and decorate with flaked almonds.

11: Pickles & Preserves

Jewish people adore their pickles. They form a major part of the traditional diet and were needed to preserve food from summer to summer. Who could imagine a salt beef sandwich without a dill pickle, or a piece of gefilte fish without chraine? These delicious additions can be made at home and the results are fabulous.

Chraine

I first made this for Pesach. It's easy with a food-processor, and the results are glorious. I will never buy it again.

Makes 1 x 250ml jar

3 medium beetroot, scrubbed
1 x 7cm piece of fresh horseradish, peeled and roughly chopped
2 tablespoons cider vinegar or balsamic vinegar
1 tablespoon olive oil
2 teaspoons salt
1 teaspoon caster sugar
1 garlic clove, peeled (optional)

1 x 250ml wide-necked jar, sterilised

Boil the whole beetroot until tender; drain and peel. Place all the ingredients in a food-processor and blitz to a smooth paste. Spoon into sterilised jar and store in the fridge for up to 6 weeks. Double or triple the quantities if you wish.

Mervyn's Garden Chutney (P)

This glorious chutney evolved out of a need to use masses of my husband Merv's garden crops that all arrived at the same time. The fruity flavour is complemented by Indian spices – and the Hairy Bikers adored their jars!

Makes 7–8 x 500ml jars

2kg tomatoes – can be squashy
3–4kg windfall apples, peeled, cored, chopped and brown parts removed
3 large onions, finely chopped
1.1 litres apple cider vinegar
175g fairtrade soft dark brown sugar
1 tablespoon coriander seeds
1 tablespoon cumin seeds
175g raisins
150g chopped dates
1 cinnamon stick
1 x 2.5cm piece of fresh root ginger, grated
1 teaspoon mustard seeds
1 small chilli, deseeded and finely chopped (optional)

7–8 x 500ml jars, sterilised

Skin the tomatoes by dropping them into a bowl of boiling water for a few minutes and then slipping off the skins. Place the skinned tomatoes, apples and onions in a large, heavy-based pan. Pour over the vinegar and add the sugar. Place over a medium heat and stir well to dissolve the sugar.

Meanwhile, place the coriander seeds and cumin seeds in a dry frying pan and toast over a low heat until they release their aroma. Grind in a pestle and mortar and add to the pan. Add the rest of the ingredients to the pan and stir gently as everything comes to the boil. Turn down the heat and simmer for 15–20 minutes, stirring occasionally, until the mixture thickens. Ladle into warm, sterilised jars and put on the lids immediately. Store in a dark cupboard and eat within 12 months. Enjoy with cheese or meat.

Dill Pickles

As a child I remember my late mother's rows of pickles sitting proudly like soldiers around her kitchen walls. In this recipe, the process may seem complicated but it will preserve the pickles for up to a year. Take care: extra chillies means extra strength and the longer you leave them – ha, if that's possible – the more intense the flavour.

Makes 3 x 1 litre jars

1kg large cucumbers
450ml good-quality cider vinegar
35g fairtrade soft light brown sugar
4 tablespoons pickling spice
5 garlic cloves, peeled and cut into large slivers
2 tablespoons caraway seeds
3 whole chillies (optional)
30g salt
25g fresh dill

3 x 1-litre wide-necked jars, sterilised in a low oven

To make the pickling liquid, place all the ingredients, except the cucumbers and dill, in a large, heavy-based pan. Pour over 1.5 litres water and bring to the boil. Put a lid on the pan and simmer for 5 minutes. Set aside to cool completely.

Meanwhile, peel the cucumbers and cut into 2cm slices on the diagonal. Break the dill into large fronds. Fill the sterilised jars with the cucumber slices and dill and pour over the cooled pickling liquid. Fasten the lids.

Place an old tea towel in the base of a large saucepan. Put your filled jars inside and fill the pan with boiling water so that it comes three-quarters of the way up the sides of the jars. Set over a lowish heat and simmer for 45–50 minutes. (This process will cook the cucumbers and also create a vacuum to preserve them.) Switch off the heat and leave the jars to cool in the liquid.

Store where people can admire! Once opened, store in the fridge.

Pickled Red Cabbage

Makes 1 litre jar

1 large, firm red cabbage
4 tablespoons salt
Either 1 litre ready-spiced vinegar or 1 litre malt vinegar and
  1 tablespoon pickling spice

1 x 1 litre jar, sterilised in a low oven

If you are making your own spiced vinegar, simmer the malt vinegar with the pickling spice in a large pan. Leave to cool, and then strain.

Remove the outer leaves of the cabbage and discard. Shred the cabbage, cutting it into 5mm slices, and wash thoroughly. Dry on kitchen paper.

Place the shredded cabbage in a large bowl and sprinkle over the salt. Cover with a tea towel and set aside to stand overnight.

Drain the cabbage through a colander and pack into your sterilised jars. Top up with the spiced vinegar and put on the lids.

Store in a cool dark place for at least week and use as required. (Use within 4 months.) Serve with cold meat or fish. Enjoy!

Lemon Curd

This makes a glorious gift presented in a decorative jar. Add a parcel label attached with a recipe for lemon-curd tarts, for style and originality.

Makes 3 x 500ml jars

3 large unwaxed lemons (organic, if possible)
240g butter or low-fat margarine, melted
450g fairtrade soft brown sugar
10 organic free-range eggs, beaten

3 x 500ml jam jars, sterilised

Grate the zest of the lemons into a glass mixing bowl and squeeze in the juice through a strainer to remove any pips. Add the butter and sugar and place over a pan of gently simmering water. Stir gently until the sugar dissolves and then add the eggs. Keep stirring until the mixture thickens, and then pour into warm, sterilised jars and put on the lids to seal.

Dried Apricot Jam

My dear late mother-in-law gave me this recipe one Passover. I've treasured it ever since.

Makes 4–5 x 500ml jars

450g dried apricots
grated zest and juice of 1 lemon
1.8 litres warm water
1.8kg granulated sugar

4–5 x 500ml jam jars, sterilised

Chop the fruit into large chunks and place in a large bowl. Pour over 1.8 litres warm water, cover the bowl with a tea towel and leave to soak for 24 hours.

The following day, pour the mixture into a large, heavy-based pan and bring to the boil. Turn down the heat and simmer for 30 minutes. Add the lemon zest and juice and sugar and stir well over a low heat until the sugar dissolves. Turn up the heat and bring to the boil. Boil rapidly for about 20–30 minutes until the jam reaches setting point. To test, drop a teaspoon onto a cold saucer. Return the saucer to the fridge for a minute or so then check if the jam is firm to the touch. If so, your jam is ready. Pour into warm, sterilised jars, put on the lids while still hot and label with pride!

Religious Aspects of Jewish Food

It may be difficult to understand some aspects of Judaism, especially when it comes to preparing and serving food. For this reason, these brief notes might be helpful. All aspects of Jewish life are governed by laws, for which the overall name is 'halakha' or 'halacha', sometimes also described as 'the path' or 'the way of walking'. Jewish food is controlled by the laws of Kashrut, which include the killing, harvesting, washing and preparation of food. Once meat has been killed, according to the law it has to be koshered by soaking and salting (except for liver, see opposite) so that all traces of blood are removed. Only fish with fins and scales may be eaten; shellfish are strictly forbidden. All fruit and vegetables must be checked for insects. Fish is never served on the same plate as meat. And milk or dairy foods are never served with a meat meal. This even applies to a cup of milky tea or coffee at the end of a meal. After a meat meal, a cup of black coffee or a glass of tea with lemon is traditional and welcome, especially with extra sugar lumps.

Food served on the Sabbath is cooked in advance as no cooking is allowed on the Sabbath or on the Fast day. A little cooking is allowed on the High Holidays, but usually a minimum. For this reason, Sabbath food is either kept hot on a blech (a heated surface), in a very low oven which stays on all night or is served cold. This is how some of the glorious cholents and tzimmes emerged from religious necessity.

During Shavuot, when milk meals are often preferred as it is a time of purity, tea or coffee with milk can be served at the end of a meal. Many of the recipes in this book have been labelled with a P which means Parve (or Parev), indicating that they are neutral and can be served with either a milk or a meat meal. Some recipes have also been adapted to use soya margarine or soya milk, such as the pastry or many of the cakes and desserts. These are also preferred by people who are lactose intolerant or watching their cholesterol, so it can be useful for health reasons.

During Passover no leaven grains can be used, so flour substitutes must be used, which are challenging. Matzo meal is available in cake, fine and medium grindings and these are used either with or without potato flour. Separating and whisking eggs also adds lightness.

Jewish Dietary Laws Demystified

Kashrut comes from the Hebrew root Kaf-Shin-Resh, which means fit, proper or correct. The word kosher can be used in its place. The reason Jews follow their kosher laws is that they are told in the Torah to obey G-d and his laws, so the dietary laws are an integral part of the Jewish religion. It is also said that the dietary laws maintain good health and self discipline.

Simple rules

Animals can only be eaten if they have cloven hooves and chew the cud – so goats, sheep, cattle, deer and bison are kosher. No other animals are permitted. Any derivative of forbidden animals – such as camel milk, lardons of bacon or camel's cheese – is also strictly forbidden.

Fish and shellfish – Things that exist in the water are only permitted if they have fins and scales, such as carp, salmon, herring and tuna-type varieties. Flatfish such as sole and plaice are permitted, but it is wise to check as fish such as swordfish and monkfish are forbidden. These days Jews will also consider those fish that have been responsibly sourced. All shellfish, such as oysters, shrimp, lobsters, crabs, and so on are forbidden.

Birds – Forbidden birds are listed within the Torah and include scavengers and birds of prey. Permitted birds include ducks, chickens, geese and turkeys. (Some very religious people do not include turkeys as they are not mentioned in the Torah, but this is not surprising as turkeys are natural inhabitants of the Americas.)

'Winged swarming things' are not permitted, though in some communities locusts can be eaten.

Leviticus does not allow amphibians, rodents, reptiles and insects, apart from the above.

Kosher slaughter – Animals may not be eaten if they died of natural causes, were killed by other animals, were road kill, or if they have suffered from diseases or health problems. Every animal must be killed by ritual slaughter. (This law does not apply to fish). Meat must be purchased from a kosher butcher.

Salting and koshering the animal to drain the blood – As Jews are not permitted to eat blood, these days most kosher butchers soak and salt the meat to remove all traces of blood. The exception is liver, which is grilled over an open flame until all the blood has been removed. Kidneys are forbidden.

Hindquarters – In most cases butchers will not purge the hindquarter's nerves and adjoining blood vessels as it takes a long time and beomes prohibitively expensive. Therefore, usually only the front quarter of the animal is used for kosher meat.

Eggs should be broken in a glass to examine for blood spots. If one is discovered the egg should be discarded and the glass washed before continuing.

Fruit and vegetables – All fruit and vegetables are kosher, but they must be examined for insects. Lettuces, cauliflower, strawberries and raspberries are particularly prone to insects so should be carefully examined, and are sometimes not permitted when catering for large numbers. Strictly religious Jews will only drink Kosher wine and other grape products.

Meat and milk – Separate cooking utensils, crockery and cutlery are required for milk and meat foods. And again for Passover foods, another whole group of milk and meat, crockery, cutlery and utensils must be used.

When eating these foods, Exodus specifies that an animal 'must not be boiled in its mother's milk'. Meat and milk foods cannot be served at the same meal. A period of time (3–6 hours) should elapse after eating a meat meal before consuming anything milky. Meat and fish must not be served together, although fish and dairy are permitted and eggs and dairy are fine. From all these laws we understand the words, *Milchig* (milky) *Fleishig* (meaty) and *Parve* (neutral).

Passover laws – These forbid the use of ordinary flour or anything that might rise and swell. This includes most grains, such as barley and wheat. In most cases, a proportion of potato flour and ground nuts, or a combination of those plus a type of matzo meal, will substitute adequately but not always perfectly. Ashkenazi and Sephardi communities disagree on the use of kitniot during Passover – rice, lentils, peas, beans and corn. These details should be checked when creating Passover meals.

Glossary

Ashkenazi – The Jews that originated in Western and Eastern Europe and Russia, as opposed to the Sephardic Jews who came from the Middle East, the Mediterranean and Asia.

Balaboster is a complimentary description of a woman who is a capable housekeeper.

Challah – A yeasted bread sometimes enriched with eggs, served on the Sabbath and festivals. The plural is challot.

Cholent and tzimmes are both stews. The Yiddish word tzimmes can also be applied to a situation of conflict or a person who is in a muddle – 'in a tzimmes'. There are vast differences between the two stews, but they both sit in the oven cooking on a slow heat from the start of the Sabbath, usually until lunchtime after synagogue the next day (respecting Jewish law, which demands that no fresh fire or heat is lit after the Sabbath).

Cholent – The word may be connected to the French word cassoulet, which describes a type of rich casserole that combines various meats and beans. Cholent was a vital element of 19th-century northern European or Ashkenazi life that began in the villages. When the Jews were confined to ghettos, the cholent became even more significant as a symbol of their Yiddishkeit or Jewishness, and songs have been devoted to its importance; it now possesses almost mystical properties. The whole of the week's food focus would centre on this Sabbath dish. As the inhabitants of the villages did not have an oven, they would send their laden pot to bake in the baker's oven after he had finished baking the special Friday challah bread. They would mark their pot in some distinctive way to set it apart from the other villagers and the contents would depend on the individual's standard of living. So, for example, if they were very poor, the basis of the pot would contain mainly potatoes and kasha (groats). But if the owner of the pot had more money, a piece of meat would be added. To make the cholent even more tempting and substantial, a layer of knaidlach or dumplings would be added to the top. These would rise to the surface with the moisture from the stew.

Falafel – A Middle-Eastern vegetarian dish made by processing soaked chickpeas with spices and cooking them in hot oil. Usually served in pitta bread with a selection of salads, hummus, tchina and a hot accompaniment such as harissa.

Gefilte fish – Traditionally, this would have been a whole lake fish with fins and scales, according to the Jewish law, served whole with the head and stuffed for the High holidays. Today, however, it describes fish forcemeat stuffing – a combination of bream, haddock and cod, mixed with chopped onions, eggs, matzo meal and seasonings. The mixture can be poached in a court bouillon or dipped in more matzo meal and fried.

Gribenes – The crackling that results from the rendered fat of poultry.

Helzel – The neck of the chicken, stuffed and roasted.

Kasha – Buckwheat groats. Barley can be substituted.

Kashrut – The Jewish dietary laws.

Knaidlach – A dumpling made out of flour or matzo meal. Used initially to extend a meat dish or soup to fill hungry stomachs, but today knaidlach are extolled for their flavour.

Knish – A filled pastry; can be made with mashed potatoes.

Kreplach – A type of triangular filled ravioli. The three corners represent Abraham, Isaac and Jacob.

Kugel – A 'set' cake-type food. Can be made from vegetables and potatoes and served with or as a meal. Kugel can also be served as a dessert, such as a lokshen kugel – a noodle cake-style pudding – one of my mother's specialities.

Lokshen – Noodles.

Rosh Hashanah – The Jewish New Year.

Traif – Food that is forbidden by Jewish law.

Yom Tov – Literally 'Good Year', but also used as a term for a festival.

Index

A

almonds
  almond drops 224
  blackcurrant and almond
    tart 143
  carrot and almond bake 204
  cinnamon macaroons 222
  Sarah Nathan's chocolate and
    almond biscuits 181
  Shabbat almond, peach and
    apple kuchen 158
  toffee'd almonds 219
  vanilla and almond kipferl 174
apples 140
  apfel im schlafrock 144
  apfel strudel 142
  apple cake 164
  Mervyn's garden chutney 231
  my mother Judith's wonderful
    apple pie 143
  Shabbat almond, peach and
    apple kuchen 158
  sticky toffee apple pudding for
    Rosh Hashanah 140
apricots
  dried apricot jam 233
artichokes 32
  artichokes with lemon
    mayonnaise 32
  Roman fried artichokes 34
asparagus
  asparagus and leek blintzes
    with Y Fenni cheese 27
  grilled asparagus soufflé 24
aubergines 14
  aubergine with eggs and
    onions 14
  baba ganoush 14
  spicy aubergine and coconut
    curry 115
avocados 17
  avocado and citrus salad 17
  avocado with ginger and chilli
    dressing 17

B

baba ganoush 14
bagels 190
baked lemon cheesecake for

Shavuot 166
baked sea bass stuffed with
  olives and herbs 77
barley
  barley tabbouleh 136
  butter bean and barley
    soup 47
  chicken and barley risotto 98
  mushroom and barley soup 45
beans
  butter bean and barley
    soup 47
beef
  liver schnitzel with red wine
    sauce 84
  meat borscht 56
  meatballs in tomato sauce 87
  oxtail cholent 85
  salt beef 82
  salt beef with knaidlach 82
  sweet and sour beef 84
beetroot
  chraine 228
  meat borscht 56
  vegetarian borscht 55
bialys 192
blackcurrant and almond
  tart 143
blintzes 148
  asparagus and leek blintzes
    with Y Fenni cheese 27
borscht 54
  meat borscht 56
  vegetarian borscht 54
bourekas 30
brandied chocolate mousse
  149
bread 182–83
  bagels 190
  bialys 192
  blinis 197
  challah 195–6
  croissants 198
  easy caraway rye 188
  granary bread 189
  onion layered focaccia 193
  pitta bread 184
  pretzels 187
bream in sweet and sour

sauce 76
buckwheat blini 197

C

cabbage
  cabbage holishkes 119
  falafel with grated cabbage
    salad 21
  hot spiced cabbage 128
  pickled red cabbage 232
  sweet and sour red cabbage
    128
caper and garlic vinaigrette 34
carrots
  carrot and almond bake 204
  carrot and honey tzimmes 126
  easy carrot, orange and olive
    oil cake 163
  Moroccan cooked carrot
    salad 137
cauliflower and onion soup 44
cauliflower pancakes 208
challah 195
  delicious challah 196
  super-rich challah 195
Chanukah 173
cheese
  asparagus and leek blintzes
    with Y Fenni cheese 27
  blintzes 148
  bourekas 30
  rich fruit and cheese roll 172
  spinach and cheesy leek
    roulade 207
cheesecake
  baked lemon cheesecake for
    Shavuot 166
chestnuts
  mushrooms and chestnuts
    in red wine sauce with fluffy
    mustard mash 129
chicken
  chicken and barley risotto 98
  chicken and rice with zhug
  chicken and wurst pie 102
  chicken tagine 102
  chopped liver 37
  DIY shawarma 104
  gribenes and schmaltz 37

Jewish penicillin Vietnamese
  style 40
  p'tcha 101
  tagliatelle frinsidisi 99
chickpeas
  falafel with grated cabbage
    salad 21
  hummus 22
  kreplach 62
chilli
  avocado with ginger and chilli
    dressing 17
chocolate
  brandied chocolate mousse
    149
  chocolate and orange dainty
    152
  chocolate, raspberry and
    cream torte 216
  date and orange chocolate
    brownies 218
  Judith's black and white cake
    156
  Pesach double chocolate
    orange cookies 219
  rich chocolate and matzo
    cake 212
  Sarah Nathan's chocolate
    and almond biscuits 181
chopped liver 37
chraine 227, 228
  pulled lamb with chraine 89
chremslach 208
cinnamon macaroons 222
citrus
  avocado and citrus salad 17
coconut
  coconut clouds 224
  coconut pyramids 221
  spicy aubergine and coconut
    curry 115
coriander
  vegetable mixed grill with mint
    and coriander dressing 122
coulibiac of smoked and fresh
  salmon 71
cream
  chocolate, raspberry and
    cream torte 216

herrings in soured cream or Greek yogurt 66
mushrooms in soured cream 18
crème brûlée, extra-easy cheat's 149
croissants 198

D
date and orange chocolate brownies 218
delicious fruit nuggets 222
desserts 139
dill pickles 232
DIY shawarma 104
doughnuts 173
doughnuts for Chanukah 173
dried apricot jam 233
duck
roast duck Polish style 106

E
easy caraway rye 188
easy carrot, orange and olive oil cake 163
easy delicious peach cobbler 151
easy red lentil soup 51
eggs 24
aubergine with eggs and onions 14
egg and onion 27
grilled asparagus soufflé 24
huevos haminados 204
shakshuka 134
sweet potato tortilla with wurst 93
essig fleisch 84
etrog drizzle cake 169
extra-easy cheat's crème brûlée 149

F
falafel with grated cabbage salad 21
farfel 60
fig rolls 179
fish 65
gefilte fish 78
Sephardi hot spiced fish 74
foragers' pie 202
fruit, dried

delicious fruit nuggets 222
rich fruit and cheese roll 172
simcha fruit cake 165

G
garlic and caper vinaigrette 34
ginger
avocado with ginger and chilli dressing 17
granary bread 189
grilled asparagus soufflé 24

H
Hairy Bikers 27, 158, 231
hamantaschen for Purim 171
healthier Jewish croissants 198
healthy yeasted blini 197
herbs
baked sea bass stuffed with olives and herbs 77
herby gnocchi in mushroom sauce 205
herrings 35
chopped herring 35
herrings in soured cream or Greek yogurt 66
soused herrings 66
homemade tomato sauce 134
honey
carrot and honey tzimmes 126
honey cake 161
hot spiced cabbage 128
huevos haminados 204
hummus 22

J
Jewish food 6, 8–9
history 10–11
religious aspects 234–5
Jewish penicillin Vietnamese style 40
Judith's black and white cake 156
Judith's wonderful apple pie 143

K
kasha
roast shoulder of lamb with kasha stuffing 88
kashrut 13, 81, 234–4
kichlach 180

knaidlach 61
salt beef with knaidlach 82
super-fluffy knaidlach 61
knishes 28
kreplach 62

L
lamb
lamb goulash 90
pulled lamb with chraine 89
roast shoulder of lamb with kasha stuffing 88
latkes 132
leeks
asparagus and leek blintzes with Y Fenni cheese 27
leek and pea pie 112
spinach and cheesy leek roulade 207
watercress and baby leek soup 42
lemons
artichokes with lemon mayonnaise 32
baked lemon cheesecake for Shavuot 166
lemon curd 233
lemon spiced gravlax 73
wafer biscuits 221
whole poached salmon with lemon sauce 72
lentils 51
easy red lentil soup 51
mujadara 136
Persian spiced lentil patties 120
Sephardi-style harira soup 52
liver schnitzel with red wine sauce 84
lokshen pudding 147

M
magic cheat's doughnuts 173
mandelbrot 177
mandelen 59
matzos
matzo balls 61
rich chocolate and matzo cake 212
meat 81
meatballs in tomato sauce 87
meringue pillows 224

Mervyn's garden chutney 231
Mervyn's roast tomato soup 48
mint
vegetable mixed grill with mint and coriander dressing 122
Moroccan cooked carrot salad 137
mujadara 136
mushrooms 18
foragers' pie 202
herby gnocchi in mushroom sauce 205
mushroom and barley soup 45
mushroom dumplings 19
mushrooms and chestnuts in red wine sauce with fluffy mustard mash 129
mushrooms in soured cream 18
mustard mash 129

N
nockerl 60
noodles
almost fat-free lokshen pudding 147
rich lokshen pudding – milk style 147
nuts
nutty Passover rolls 208
stuffed monkeys 176

O
olive oil
easy carrot, orange and olive oil cake 163
olives
baked sea bass stuffed with olives and herbs 77
onions
aubergine with eggs and onions 14
cauliflower and onion soup 44
egg and onion 27
onion layered focaccia 193
onion soup 54
spiced onion and vegetable pakoras 133
stuffed onions 118
oranges
chocolate and orange dainty 152

date and orange chocolate
brownies 218
easy carrot, orange and olive
oil cake 163
Pesach double chocolate
orange cookies 219
oxtail cholent 85

P
p'tcha 101
Passover 183, 200–1
Passover pastry 213
Passover rolls 208
Passover sponge 210
pasta
savoury vegetable and noodle
kugel 117
pastry 142
bourekas 30
wonderful Passover pastry
213
peaches
easy delicious peach cobbler
151
Shabbat almond, peach and
apple kuchen 158
super-moist Yom Tov peach
dessert cake 160
peas
leek and pea pie 112
Persian spiced lentil patties 120
Pesach double chocolate
orange cookies 219
pickles 227
dill pickles 232
pickled red cabbage 232
pitta bread 184
plava, perfect 215
poppyseed twist cake 168
potatoes 50
bourekas 30
foragers' pie 202
Haimishe potato soup 50
herby gnocchi in mushroom
sauce 205
knishes 28
latkes 132
mashed potato kugel 131
potato kugel 131
potato pompoms 131
spicy vegetable and potato
tagine 115

poultry 95
pretzels 187
pulled lamb with chraine 89
pulses 21
Purim 171

R
raspberries
chocolate, raspberry and
cream torte 216
rice
chicken and barley risotto 98
chicken and rice with zhug 96
mujadara 136
roasted butternut squash
risotto 110
Sephardi-style harira soup 52
tomato rice soup 48
rich chocolate and matzo cake
212
rich fruit and cheese roll 172
roast duck Polish style 106
roast shoulder of lamb with
kasha stuffing 88
roasted butternut squash
risotto 110
Roman fried artichokes 34
Rosh Hashanah 140

S
salmon
coulibiac of smoked and fresh
salmon 71
lemon spiced gravlax 73
salmon rissoles 68
smoking your own salmon 73
whole poached salmon with
lemon sauce 72
salsa verde
turkey schnitzel with salsa
verde 103
salt beef 82
salt beef with knaidlach 82
Sarah Nathan's chocolate and
almond biscuits 181
savoury vegetable and noodle
kugel 117
sea bass
baked sea bass stuffed with
olives and herbs 77
Sephardi hot spiced fish 74
Sephardi-style harira soup 52

Shabbat almond, peach and
apple kuchen 158
shakshuka 134
Shavuot 166
Simcha fruit cake 165
soups 38–9
soup extras 59–62
soused herrings 66
spices
kreplach 62
lemon spiced gravlax 73
Persian spiced lentil patties
120
Sephardi hot spiced fish 74
spiced onion and vegetable
pakoras 133
spicy aubergine and coconut
curry 115
spicy vegetable and potato
tagine 115
spinach
bourekas 30
spinach and cheesy leek
roulade 207
squash
roasted butternut squash
risotto 110
starters 13
sticky toffee apple pudding for
Rosh Hashanah 140
stuffed autumn vegetables 125
stuffed monkeys 176
stuffed onions 118
super-moist Yom Tov peach
dessert cake 160
sweet and sour red cabbage
128
sweet potato tortilla with
wurst 93

T
tabbouleh 136
tagliatelle frinsidisi 99
toffee apple pudding for Rosh
Hashanah 140
toffee'd almonds 219
tomatoes
homemade tomato sauce 134
meatballs in tomato sauce 87
Mervyn's garden chutney 231
Mervyn's roast tomato
soup 48

tomato rice soup 48
turkey
DIY shawarma 104
turkey schnitzel with salsa
verde 103

V
vanilla and almond kipferl 174
vegetables 109
savoury vegetable and noodle
kugel 117
spiced onion and vegetable
pakoras 133
spicy vegetable and potato
tagine 115
stuffed autumn vegetables
125
vegetable mixed grill with mint
and coriander dressing 122
vegetarian borscht 54

W
wafer biscuits 221
watercress and baby leek
soup 42
whole poached salmon with
lemon sauce 72
wine
liver schnitzel with red wine
sauce 84
mushrooms and chestnuts
in red wine sauce with fluffy
mustard mash 129
wonderful Passover pastry 213
wurst
chicken and wurst pie 102
sweet potato tortilla with
wurst 93

Y
yogurt
extra-easy cheat's crème
brûlée 149
herrings in soured cream or
Greek yogurt 66

Z
zhug
chicken and rice with zhug 96
DIY shawarma 104

Acknowledgements

I will always be grateful to Kyle who understood my vision and made my dreams come true, giving me the chance to work with her wonderful team: Catharine Robertson, my enthusiastic and superb editor; Isobel Wield, my inspired photographer; Sonja Edridge, who professionally and lovingly worked though the recipes and Sue Rowlands, who organised the props gently and efficiently. Together they have produced this wonderful book.

Sincere thanks also to Darryl Samaraweera, my agent at Artellus, for supporting me and having faith in my writing; Simon Round, my co-writer, who managed the poultry and meat chapters so well and Stephen Pollard, the editor of the Jewish Chronicle, for listening to my ideas.

And of course my special family: Mervyn, my loyal and wonderful husband; Sarah, my daughter, kitchen helper and buddy; Joe, my lovely, supportive son, along with my son-in-law Darren and my sweetest grandchildren, Jasmine and Phoebe – my favourite tasters.

Plus my good friends who loved, supported and tolerated my foodie passions and acted as tasters – I thank you all.